Possible

A Guide for Innovation

By William Barr

POSSIBLE: A Guide for Innovation

by William Barr

Copyright © 2014 by William Barr

All rights reserved

CONTENTS

EPIGRAPH – page 6

PREFACE – page 7

CHAPTER 1: THE ADVANTAGES OF INNOVATION – page 9

    Seven Ideas - 17

    The Four Ways Ideas are Used - 20

CHAPTER 2: COMMUNICATION – page 26

    Communicate the Desire for Innovation - 26

    Listen to/ Observe Customers - 34

    Use Imagery and Symbolism - 40

    Use Facilitators - 43

    Use Positive Verbal Reinforcement - 46

    Mentor/ Protege System - 47

    Cross Fertilization of Ideas - 50

CHAPTER 3: NEW THINKING – page 56

    Focused/Unfocused - 56

    Openness to Change - 58

    Accept Risk Taking - 65

    Allow Rule Breaking Thinking - 70

Relinquish Control - 73

Meditation and Reflection - 76

Align Policy for Innovation - 79

Egalitarian Values - 80

CHAPTER 4: RESOURCES – page 83

Budget Money for Innovation - 83

Reward Innovation - 88

Avoid Stereotype Hiring - 91

Employee Training - 93

Be Informed Monitor Statistics - 96

Measure Innovation - 99

Employee Continuity - 101

Listen to Employee Opinion - 103

Outside Resources - 106

CHAPTER 5: NEW ROLES FOR PEOPLE – page 111

Autonomous Groups/Cross-Functional Teams - 111

Relate Stories - 118

Stay at Optimum Group Sizes – 120

Champions - 124

Role Flexibility - 127

Bootlegging - 129

CHAPTER 6: TECHNIQUES TO GET NEW IDEAS – p. 133

Reserved Judgment: Consider All New Ideas Positively - 133

Recombine Existing Concepts - 141

Seek Many Ideas - 142

Experimentation and R&D - 146

Prototypes - 152

Change Basic Assumptions - 155

Innovation Cuing - 158

The Innovation Process - 162

The Quick Innovation Plan - 165

CHAPTER 7: THE PSYCHOLOGY – page 167

Phenomena of Psychological Creativity - 167

Features of the Creative Personality - 177

Creative Techniques - 182

Group Dynamics - 185

Imaginational Thought - 189

Anticipate/Predict the Future - 192

BIBLIOGRAPHY – page 199

All men dream; but not equally. Those who dream by night in the dusty recesses of their minds wake in the day to find that it was vanity; but the dreamers of the day are dangerous men, for they may act their dream with open eyes to make it possible.

~ **T. E. Lawrence (of Arabia)** *Seven Pillars of Wisdom*

PREFACE

As our case is new, so we must think anew, and act anew.
  ~ Abraham Lincoln, State of the Union Address

This is a book about people and the culture of change. Change means creating new things, and fortunately this is an ability given to all humankind. That means irregardless of intelligence level, all humans have been endowed with creative ability. These ideas are the building blocks of civilization. It is a give and take exchange of information between people, and it is essential that we facilitate this exchange to produce innovation.

A true desire to be innovative can lead any institution to be more creative and more innovative. In this book any references made to business will in general apply to any institution whether it be government, hospitals, or non-profit organizations.

For many people the field of computers is thought of as something that is very technical, yet the quote from Steve Wozniak "Invention, like art, is kind of an idea that can't be seen, but you've got to express it someway" talks about art and is coming from the chief designer of the first personal computer. Mr. Wozniak was the co-founder of Apple Computers, and again talks about art when he said "To me, an artistic design meant very few components doing the maximum job." Innovation is an art. It is built and crafted along the way just as any craftsman builds an artistic masterpiece or the painter paints. The innovator and the artist both have their tools and techniques they use as they constantly reassess what they do.

Economist Peter Drucker has said that "management is a practice and not a science." Innovation is not a science, rather, it is an art that must be imbued with passion by you the innovator. For those who need to innovate, this book will show the way, you just add the passion.

William Barr
Houston, Texas

CHAPTER 1: THE ADVANTAGES OF INNOVATION

If a man make a better mouse trap than his neighbor, though he build his house in the woods, the world will make a beaten path to his door. ~ Ralph Waldo Emerson (1803-1882)

Innovation is the key to improving the world.
 ~ Bill Gates, 2012 Annual Letter

Every process, every system, every product or service can be improved with innovative thinking. Any product can be made better. Every good idea that exists in one area can be applied in some way to other distinctly different areas. Good ideas are every where. First of type ideas are waiting to be discovered. During a filmed interview reporters asked the great inventor Thomas Edison about the opportunities available to young men. He paused just a moment and in a high, creaky voice answered "new inventions will never end."

Innovation is not so much a strategy as it is a way of doing things. It is a tactical decision to be flexible in developing new solutions to the ever changing demands of a market "led by an invisible hand." Core ideas can be changed on a daily basis if necessary in order to find the winning idea. An idea can be modified, increased in size, changed in a particular area, increased or decreased in speed, have ideas added to it, be imagined with unlimited resources, used with ideas from outside the business, or extrapolated and expanded in every feature or value, extending from the known to the unknown.

Alvin Toffler says in his book *Power Shift* that the world is now divided into the "fast and the slow." Efficient innovation is directly related to how fast products and services are brought to market. Obviously, the fast are the winners. Honda motorcycles, Kyocera Ceramics, and Casio calculators dominated their markets specifically because they brought more products to market more rapidly than the competition. The speed of diffusion of technology can make even high tech items like computers become commodities until they are new again.

Successful companies now realize that productivity, quality, and customer service are not the competitive advantages they were in the past; rather they are merely the basic requirement for admission to the free market place.

Systematic innovation, sustained in every aspect, is now the key to competitive advantage.

In a Watson Wyatt survey called *Innovation in the 21st Century* executives stated that one of the most important traits of future employees was an ability to create new ideas. In IBM's *2010*

Global CEO Study, creativity was selected as the most crucial factor for future success, and was more important than "rigor, management discipline, integrity or even vision."

In his usual and succinct manner, Peter Drucker has stated that "a business has only two functions: marketing and innovation." Innovation is seen in every area of life and is not just about products and services. Innovation is just anything new and useful. It can be a new product or service, but it can also be a new way to use a old idea. When aviation designer Burt Rutan first used small wings on the front of his airplane designs, it was perceived as an innovation, however, the very first successful aircraft built by the Wright Brothers used a front wing (known as a canard). It was innovative of Rutan to apply a concept that had not been used for over a half century. Thomas Edison said to "keep on the lookout for novel ideas that others have used successfully. Your idea has to be original only in its adaption to the problem you're working on." An innovation can be in the way something is applied or used, or facilitating a unique human interaction, or process, or use of material, or social interpretation, or anything new. The effects of innovation cover a wide spectrum. It can be an incremental effect all the way through a spectrum to something that upsets the status quo; a disruptive technology or "paradigm shift" a term popularized by Thomas Kuhn in his 1962 book *The Structure of Scientific Revolutions.* The following list is some examples of innovations in different areas:

1. Technology (transistor, LASER).

2. Societal practices (HMO's, Welfare, no fault insurance).

3. Manufacturing (mass production, robotics, re-engineering).

4. Governmental policies (Medicare and Social Security).

5. Management (management by walking around, management by objective).

6. Financial (installment buying).

7. Patterns of human interaction (house husband, contract marriages).

8. Entertainment (Internet, satellite TV, smart phones, Wii console).

9. Information diffusion (Social media, LAN computing, cards with medical information an a computer chip, bar codes, QR codes, the Internet, RFID tags).

10. Labor practices (Employee quality control groups, cross-functional teams).

11. Marketing and strategy (Perrier water as a cocktail, life style marketing, sharing knowledge with competitors, or giving products or services away free).

12. Distribution of products and services (banks in supermarkets, McDonald's in a gas station).

13. Image (Pepsi's youth generation, U.S. Army's "Be all you can be").

14. Materials (plastics, ceramics, recycling, intelligent materials, nano materials).

For years now the leaders of business have been telling the world just how important innovation is to us all. The president of the National Academy of Engineering, Robert M. White told them "invention- and inventors- are as critical to the advancement of our nation's economic growth in the 1990's as they were in what we sometimes think of as the Golden Age of Invention in the 1890's" (*Vital Speeches*). He also said "inventions are the lifeblood coursing through the heart of industrial competitiveness."

In an article by Allan R. Taylor, Chairman and Chief Executive Officer of the Royal Bank of Canada (*Vital Speeches*) he refers to the industrial age and the information age, and he says now we are in "The Age of Ideas" (The Nomura Research Institute calls it "creation intensification" or the "age of brain-ware.") Taylor places great importance on innovation and states "I want to emphasize today. We must understand that, ideas, innovation, inventions, and entrepreneurship - supported by appropriate education, and training - are the real engines of growth in creating the wealth of nations." Mr. Taylor points out significant work done by Dr. Paul Romer a professor of economics at New York University who links the production of ideas to economic growth. He was named one of the 25 most influential Americans by *Time* magazine in 1997. Romer says ideas are the "critical engines of growth," and George T. Land says in his book *Grow or Die* that "information is the fuel of the engine."

The creativity and ideas for success are within the companies already. An M.I.T. Sloan School of Management study showed that 85% of 39 innovators that left a Massachusetts company were still successful after 5 years. These 33 had combined sales two times the sales of the company they left. Companies are buying other companies to obtain their intellectual capital, and Dow Chemical uses what they call IAM or intellectual asset management. Ideas are the real basis of business today. This is exemplified by the stock market value of Microsoft with only $69 Billion in sales (2011), being greater than the stock market value of General Motors which had $150 Billion in sales per year (2011). Microsoft is more valuable than GM because Microsoft's ideas are more valuable. A *New York Times* magazine cover story stated "Microsoft's only factory asset is the human imagination."

Failure to be innovative can have dire consequences for businesses. International Harvester lost 1.64 billion dollars in 1982 while in the same period their competitor Caterpillar remained profitable by keeping innovative with new services such as guaranteed delivery of parts within 24 hours.

Companies need to rapidly innovate new products and services to meet a global, international market demand. Co-founder and CEO of AST Research in Irvine, California was Safi Qureshey. In an Inc. magazine article he wryly commented "The computer business is changing so quickly these days that sometimes we feel as if we're in the fresh-produce business." In a rapidly transforming world, companies need to learn how to become experts at "continuous change."

SOME OF THE ADVANTAGES OF INNOVATION ARE:

1. Only you have it. This is Total Advantage.

2. An innovation is more valuable because of its newness. It is of greater value to the user because of the increased advantage the user has compared to their competitors who don't have the innovation. A business that has the use of an innovation is receiving increased competitive advantage. The more efficient Toro lawn aerator outsold the competition 2 to 1. This increased value to the user means you can make a premium profit.

3. You may be able to obtain long term rights to ownership with patents, copyrights, formulas, salesmarks, or trademarks. Other ownership rights may apply. Many companies now claim ownership to a "look".

4. You can get free advertising with press releases to newspapers, magazines, websites, and discussion on social forums because you have something new.

5. Because it is something new you get a powerful, extremely persuasive type of free advertising: word of mouth.

6. Innovation creates the real perception of leadership. This lends respect to the other things you do, and clearly identifies you as a leader in your area of business. Because you are a leader, people will be more likely to consider your product and services, giving

you further opportunity. Even though American Airlines' frequent flyer program is essentially the same as other programs, more people use theirs because they were the innovator and they are perceived as the leader in this area.

7. It is an indicator of the company's health. In *Managing for the Future* by Peter Drucker he states that a company not innovating is in decline.

8. As the product/service gets older you will have regained the initial R & D costs and will be able to reduce the price enough to defeat the competition. DuPont did this with Nylon. Analyst David Soetebier at A.G. Edwards in St. Louis says "The company that comes out with a product first has greater profitability throughout the products life." The innovator is always further down the learning curve and with any diligence the innovator is always ahead of the competition.

Toffler also states in *Power Shift* that "knowledge is the crux of tomorrow's worldwide struggle for power," however he does not refute Einstein who said "imagination is more important than knowledge" (Einstein *On Science*) because with imagination we obtain new knowledge. Whether history will look back on these days as the "Age of Ideas" or the "Information Age" we are indeed living during a revolutionary time.

SEVEN IDEAS

In order to reap the advantages of innovation, seven fundamental ideas must be applied to your business. First, you must have a distinct awareness about the advantage itself and believe that this is the most important strategy your business can adopt for its long term success and profitability. Studies have shown that just investing money in innovation does not produce the best results, rather, it is a combination of two ideas: a simple attitude change in the culture of your company, plus the investment that gives the best results. Even though Apple used one of the smallest percentages of sales for their R & D (2.2% in 2011), they are considered one of the most innovative companies in the world, the result of a high culture of innovation.

Secondly, innovation must become a permanent feature in the company's communications, and this is not something that only management is doing, rather it is a feature of every part of the business.

Thirdly, new and very distinct patterns of thinking must be established which will be the thoughts that proceed creative action. Change of the status quo must be embraced like an old friend and it should be something this is encountered with excitement and passion. Change can be dealt with effectively by using planning and preparation, and should be moving toward some ideal and future world.

The fourth idea is to use every single resource you have available, and this is not just money or people but whatever resource you can turn to you advantage in developing innovative ideas. The model that best describes the innovative business requires the maximum use of all employees to produce the greatest amount of ideas.

Fifth, you must see people acting in new roles that go outside the boundaries that normally described what they did and how they did it. There must seemingly be a state of chaos for awhile. The Greek poet Hesiod (750 to 675 B.C.) wrote in *Birth of the Gods* "Chaos was born first." Mary Shelley, author of the novel *Frankenstein* said "Invention, it must be admitted, does not consist of creating out of void but out of chaos." A long period of study, preparation, and stimulating discussion must occur which crosses boundaries and proceeds innovation.

Sixth, certain techniques must be used just as tools are used by an artist. These techniques increase the results from your efforts and can be any idea which you find to be effective. Computer software such as that available from www.invention-machine.com can also aid in your search for new ideas. (Their patent #5,901,068 claims to accelerate innovation).

The seventh idea is the most important change to your thinking that will cause increased levels of innovation. It is an awareness of the importance of the individual. The most fundamental mistake being made by almost all business today is limiting the use of ideas from only the company's leader or its management. This prejudice is mirrored in the area of training where we see the most training being given to management. An assumption of sorts has been made that the greater skills of the manager is more deserving of nourishment or attention. The creative act preceding innovation is more about uniqueness and the unique perspective of the individual. It was the unique perspective of a Idaho farm boy who created the idea of the all electronic scanning television, a system superior to earlier attempts at TV designs. Philo Farnsworth saw the row after row of plowed fields on his family farm as rows of electronic scanning lines and first brought his idea to his high school teacher. On September 3, 1928 he demonstrated his TV to the press and eventually licensed his patents to RCA. Without an engineering degree or an MBA this farm boy's unique perspective created the first successful TV system, a pivotal development that changed the world. *Time* magazine named Farnsworth one of the top 100 most important people of the 20th century.

At Pixar, the talent behind the animated movie *Toy Story*, executive Pam Kerwin said "everyone's opinion was expected." It is imperative that the innovative organization gets as many ideas as possible and therefore must use all its employees and their unique view of reality. Author John Steinbeck wrote "Once the miracle of creation has taken place, the group can build and extend it, but the group never invents anything. The preciousness lies in the lonely mind of a man." Corporate culture must facilitate innovation, and it starts at the level of the individual where the creation of a new idea is born.

THE FOUR WAYS IDEAS ARE USED

Basically, ideas are used four different ways. One way is they can be used as proprietary property including patents, copyrights, and trademarks. Secondly, you can use ideas in total secret. Thirdly, is to use ideas faster than anyone else, and the fourth way is to share ideas with others.

There has been an accelerating trend (7 to 8% increase per year) amongst businesses to develop and own patents, trademarks, and copyrighted material including recipes and formulas (6,478 patents obtained by IBM in 2012 including those for cognitive computing; computers that learn).

The 2012 top ten list for U.S. Patent awards is:
1. IBM   6,478 (20th consecutive year at #1 position)
2. Samsung   5,081
3. Canon   3,174

4. SONY 3,032
5. Panasonic 2,769
6. Microsoft 2,613
7. Toshiba 2,447
8. Hon Hai 2.013
9. General Electric 1,652
10. LG Electronics 1,624

Either you gain competitive advantage by using the ideas exclusively or you can license others, giving your company financial advantage. It is management's responsibility to decide what should be patented. If you ask a lawyer they will want to patent everything because that's what they do, however, you must pay them to do this. A basic patent costs between $7,000 and $15,000 and design patents are from $2,500 to $4,000. The attorney will automatically make the broadest claims possible and then spend years in court defending them; and you must pay them. It is not the attorney's fault if money is wasted for a patent you will never use, because they are doing their job. It is your job to decide what to patent, keeping in mind that markets can transform rapidly. Patent ideas of great benefit and usefulness to you, and claim just what is truly unique and beneficial to your company. This way you will have a strong position that is less likely to be challenged in court (note the expensive patent wars between Apple, Samsung, and Google in 2012). It is also a scientific fact that humans have only so much "psychological focus" and can be needlessly distracted by long litigation battles. Additionally, it has been shown that other companies can very often design around your patent idea (Mansfield et al., 1981). Thomas Edison eventually patented 1,093 ideas and obtained 2,332 patents worldwide, and at the same time he called patent litigation "the suicide of time."

A second way is to use your ideas in secret, and companies such as Apple and Google are famous for their secrecy. New employees might be hired and not even know what they'll be working on. The company store at Apple offers a T-shirt that says "I visited the Apple Campus, but that's all I'm allowed to say." Apple co-founder and CEO Steve Jobs had a legendary temper and would warn employees that failure to keep secrets at Apple could mean termination (just losing your job … I think). Keeping things secret means all your employees should sign confidentiality agreements, and necessarily so because the innovative company is seeking ideas from all its employees. Any advantageous idea you have in any area can be kept secret giving you an edge over your competition. For Apple, secrecy creates anticipation about products and gives a feeling of mystery to the company.

Somethings are totally secret, while others can be in the open but your competition doesn't realize what you're doing, your reasons remaining secret. Walmart was eventually recognized by analysts for being innovative in the sophisticated use of computers in purchasing. Once a supplier was hired and entered into the system, Walmart never ordered anything again. Suppliers were allowed access to the Walmart computers and fulfilled orders as they determined a need existed. This eliminated a tremendous amount of work by Walmart purchasing personnel, saving large amounts of money for Walmart, and was better for the supplier because they were better able to judge their own production needs. Many other companies have adopted this idea.

A third way that ideas are used is to use ideas faster than anyone else. Ideas can still be patented, but this method generally precludes obtaining a patent (once an idea becomes public knowledge it cannot be patented) the idea being to reap the most benefits from the idea before the competition is able to enter the market, and before the next new idea appears. Because ideas are developing faster in today's world, Bill Gates told the *Wall Street Journal* "Intellectual property has the shelf life of a banana." Develop ideas in secret and then use ideas in secret for as long as possible. This allows you to be further along the learning curve compared to the competition. You always position yourself as the leader in the market in the eyes of the consumer, always leaving competitors in a "catch up" position. Because you are perceived by consumers as the innovation leader they will want to look at your other products and services giving you further opportunity. You find the best ways to market the product or service first, picking the "low hanging fruit" and operating at a premium profit before the competition enters the market. Even when copied, by being constantly ahead of your competitors on the learning curve, you've learned how to most efficiently produce and market the innovation and have already recouped your initial investment. Now, you can even offer a more competitive price and still make a premium profit. Those businesses that compete under the old business model very often end up selling their products and services on a slim profit margin, whereas companies that seek the innovation advantage operate with the same basic expenses, while making the maximum fair profit. DuPont did this when they defeated the "Johnnie come lately" competition that tried to cash in on their creation of nylon, first used for toothbrushes (1938) and nylon stockings (1940). DuPont had recouped their initial investment and were able to crush the competition with a better product and lower price while still remaining profitable.

A fourth method for using ideas is to allow others to share in their use. IBM shared millions of dollars of software with the open source Linux movement and received benefits in financial savings and new business. When other businesses add in their creativity and effort it just makes the "whole" that much better. Google's open source platform for Android® allowed others to rapidly develop applications and subsequently Android became very successful. It's a judgment when to share, however, it will be at a point where you have a product or service that is far ahead of everyone else, and benefits from sharing seem obvious and more pragmatic. In the early days of the automobile industry the Motor Vehicle Manufacturers Association formed to allow the sharing of patents between auto builders. This allowed every company to offer a satisfactory product and benefited them and the people buying cars. Open collaboration between researchers led to the creation of the Internet and a revolution in information sharing. TED's (Technology, Entertainment and Design) Chris Anderson refers to what he calls" crowd accelerated innovation" a phenomena of the interaction and sharing on the Internet where users rapidly build on each others' ideas.

Chapter 1 – Notes:

CHAPTER 2: COMMUNICATION

COMMUNICATE THE DESIRE TO INNOVATE

I have always been driven to buck the system, to innovate, to take things beyond where they've been.
~ Sam Walton, founder of Walmart

Transmit ideas from one division to another with the speed of light. ~ Jack Welch, Previous CEO of General Electric

Firstly, there should be a clear understanding that the desire to innovate is a personal desire of the leader of the company. It will be a challenging job. The French military and political leader Napoleon Bonaparte said "I have conceived of many plans, but I was never free to execute one of them. For all that I held the rudder, and with a strong hand, the waves were always a good deal stronger." Don Frey who became vice president of development at Ford during the '60's said "nothing puts greater drag on innovation than the inertia in your own organization" (*Harvard Business Review.*)

A 1951 British movie called *The Man in the White Suit* starring Alec Guinness, was about a British chemist at a textile mill who invents a near indestructible fabric (it has to be cut with a blow torch) that repels dirt. At first everyone thinks it will be a product that will be the best thing since sliced bread. Then a rich industrialist from a competing mill tries to buy the rights to it in order to suppress it because "who will need new material?" They shout fearfully about how it will upset the market and all the supporting industries. The strongest argument against Progress is finally made when an old wash woman says she will lose her job (the fabric repels dirt) "you scientists, when will you stop meddling with things?" Resistance to change will be enormous, however the final analysis is the company must follow change and innovate to compete with Time, and the leadership of a company must be sure in this conviction.

In the *Vital Speeches* June 1, 1993 issue the President and CEO of Conoco (an energy company) Constantine S. Nicandros gave a speech titled *The Innovation Imperative*. He states that innovation is "a state of mind throughout an organization, from top to bottom." At times events will warrant revising the vision, so it will be a continuous process. It is a innovation process that must be done with passion and daring using "a state of mind" and includes absolutely everyone in the company "from top to bottom."

The importance of clearly communicating the vision of innovation was indicated by a study performed at Bell Laboratories in 1990. A *Harvard Business Review* article called

How Bell Labs Creates Star Performers by Robert Kelly of Carnegie Mellon University, and management consultant Janet Caplan, showed that the communication of a clear vision increased productivity. When people clearly know what it is they are supposed to do, then they are more productive in reaching their goals. It is extremely important that the leadership of the company clearly defines the core values of the company so that the employees can "stay on track." This vision must be effectively communicated while still allowing flexibility in exactly how it will be implemented, allowing people to add in their own creativity. President John Kennedy did this when he said "I believe that this nation should commit itself to achieving the goal, before this decade is out, of landing a man on the moon and returning him safely to Earth." New miniaturized electronics and other great innovations were the result of Kennedy's challenge to America.

The CEO and the company's management should communicate a desire to innovate using three essential techniques: the actions it takes; its verbal communications; and by using written/visual communications. In this way the CEO will be acting as an artist, constantly reassessing and recreating.

Actions include things such as creating specific groups to facilitate innovation, creating specific funds for innovation, creativity training, or the purchase of something which would be used to facilitate innovation. In other words, don't just talk about it, do it; take action.

Verbal communications means management is talking about innovation and verbally encouraging it. The CEO should make a speech about innovation, and must clearly articulate the need to facilitate it. The upper levels of management must understand they will be giving employees greater flexibility in the way they operate, and greater responsibility. Upper management should articulate the goals of innovation by describing a verbal vision of what the company is trying to accomplish. (This vision should be about something other than profits). Words and phrases related to innovation should enter the company vocabulary. General Electric used the slogan "Progress is our most important product" and Rico Copiers used the slogan "Where imagination becomes reality." Panasonic had a slogan "Create the future." 3M used "innovation working for you." Lockheed Aircraft used "Giving shape to imagination." Other examples include using phrases such as "break through ideas," or "leading edge thinking" or "creative solutions" or other language which clearly relates to innovation. Also, other language should be used which challenges the employees to be creative and encourages their curiosity.

Rounding out an effective communication is the third method, the written word and visual material. This includes normal communications such as inter-office memos and letters. Also, the use of brochures, newsletters, and video related to innovation are important communications. A newsletter could be created that would be wholly devoted to innovation in the company. This can also be done with email or internal company websites. Allow management to take turns as editors and have guest writers. Video can be used in various ways such as a personal message from the CEO or others in the company leadership, that talks about innovation. Multiple copies can be distributed through out the company to be used on a repeated basis and for new employees. Video can be used to graphically show a group of possible creative solutions which might then be tested, or as a stimulus to further thinking. Posters can also be used to remind people of the company's desire to innovate.

It is important too that not only is the idea of innovation communicated, it must be understood. It is managements' job to see that the goal and vision of innovation is something that the employees see themselves as a part of, and instrumental in their own self actualization. There must be open, frank, and frequent expression of the company's values, goals, and vision. Ask employees at all levels to be supportive of each others ideas and explain how innovation will work to improve the company. Explain to the employees how an innovative company will provide better job security because it will help insure the success of the company. An innovative company will also be a more interesting place for them to work. Discuss the employees part in the practice of innovation and how this is part of the company's goals.

It is a feature of communication in general, that a deterioration in belief and a reduction in the extent of meaning will occur if the communication is not repeated on a regular basis. If there is no repetition, then soon the people will believe the communicator did not really have a strong position, or did not truly believe in what they were saying, or other reasons to disbelief the communicator, and they will begin to reduce the extent of the meaning. They will do this by thinking the communication was not to be applied in every area, or for a long period of time, or in every detail, or other ways to reduce the extent of the meaning. Therefore, because it has been said once that the company desires to be innovative, it should not be assumed the importance originally attributed to this communication will remain at a high level. The desire to innovate must be communicated on a regular basis, and the language relating to it should always remain a significant part of the company's vocabulary. IBM developed a 22 page booklet for employees called "Your Ideas Have Value." Not only is this an effective way to communicate the company's desire to be creative, it also helps explain how the employee can be apart of the company's vision. Their ability to see themselves as a part of what the company is trying to accomplish is a great motivator. It is important that the company continues to emphasize its vision and how innovation is a part of that vision.

Interestingly, companies in the book *In Search Of Excellence* (Peters & Waterman) whose goals were other than money (that is, the Vision) were more successful. This vision to innovate must be communicated, and it is the chief responsibility of the CEO. Warren Bennis in his book *Leaders* found in every instance, the 90 successful leaders he studied were the prime movers and architects of the companies vision. It is the CEO's chief responsibility to be describing the corporate vision, and you should also have a written vision statement. For example, General Motors vision statement says " GM's vision is to be the world leader in transportation products and related services, and we will earn our customers' enthusiasm through continuous improvement driven by the integrity, teamwork, and the innovation of GM people."

Frequently, what the leadership talks about must include some direct or indirect reference to innovation or creativity. Many times it must be something that is idealistic and far reaching so that the members of the company have some room to stretch themselves intellectually. In other words they need room to add in their own creativity. This vision must include perspective, direction, observation, and introspection. It must be a broad field of view that sees all the way to the horizon, and what novelist Ayn Rand called an "borrowed vision." In a 1936 *Ford Dealer* article, Henry Ford wrote "There will be changes for the better in almost every part of the car" and he expected "to see synthetic substitutes for some of our metals." Ford was looking ahead to a distant future, and yet this could have been accomplished in a much closer future than he was anticipating. There now exists an accelerating realization of possibilities.

The message of innovation is also something that is going to be communicated to your customer through your direct contact and through the media. Everything new about what you offer should be told, and because curiosity is an inherent trait in humans, anything new stands a good chance of being tried out by the consumer. Make sure this is something truly new because consumers are beginning to doubt some of the claims. The terms "innovative" "new" and "innovation" have been used for some things that are just minor changes.

Again, in order to assure a powerful instruction to your people, all three essential communication methods must be used; actions, written/visual, and verbal. This need to communicate the leadership's desire for the company to be creative and innovative, is the initial act which will energize the company toward innovation. The more powerfully this is communicated, the greater will be the resulting creativity which proceeds innovation. The members of your organization have the ability to be innovative, but the vast majority need to be given psychological permission (as absurd as that sounds) and encouragement. The importance of communicating the desire to innovate is something that must be emphasized here because the degree of importance is more significant than most people will understand intuitively. All innovation in your company follows from this potentially forceful communication.

Executive Vice President of the Chase Manhattan Bank, A. Wright Elliott gave a speech called Creativity and Enterprise (*Vital Speeches*) in which he said "Collective innovation in any enterprise swells up from below....but, it is made possible by the quality of vision at the top... vision which acts as a magnetic force to pull the organization forward."

LISTEN TO/ OBSERVE CUSTOMERS

Know and understand the customer so well the product or service fits him and sells itself. ~ Peter Drucker

Spend a lot of time talking to customers face to face. You'd be amazed how many companies don't listen to their customers.
 ~ Ross Perot, legendary American businessman

Apparently, individuals outside of commercial industry are the leaders in producing new, basic, first of type ideas. In a study by Ralph Landau (*Chemical Industry Research & Innovation*, from Innovation & Research Symposium 129, American Chemical Society) made of the chemical process industry over the last 25 years, out of 31 major breakthroughs, 22 came from outside of the chemical process industry. That is a very significant majority of 71 percent!

Even though Samuel P. Langley (1834-1906) was heavily funded by the United States government to produce a flying machine, it was the Wright brothers who on their own built the world's first successful powered aircraft.

The Technical Assistance Research Programs Institute of Washington D.C. conducted studies which confirmed the following: 25% of consumers in America would use a different business than the one they were using because of dissatisfaction. Out of that 25%, only 5% of customers would complain to the business or indicate why they were dissatisfied. Almost a fourth of American consumers were walking out of businesses with the intention of going somewhere else next time! In many cases, creative problem solving would lead to a variety of innovations in service and product if only the business would listen to the customer.

In a study of scientific instruments by Eric Von Hippel of M.I.T. all the instruments that were first of a type were invented by the users (called lead users). Even in the area of major improvements, 85% of the innovations came from the users, and users accounted for 66% of even incremental improvements! This would seem to indicate one of two things; either business has a great deal of room for improvement in original innovation, or the great advantage for business is in the area of small innovations. In the semiconductor and electronic process equipment industry, users developed 100% of the first of type innovations used commercially. Von Hippel suggests a systematic approach to find lead users: through networking, by looking for users in similar fields of work, and by examining any true leaders on the cutting edge of new use.

The Japanese have been very successful in the area of incremental improvement, and John Sealy Brown at Xerox has talked about incremental improvements. Sometimes this is a small, simple thing a user discovers. Procter and Gamble started in 1837 in the soap business. It was from their customers that they learned their soap floated and the customers kept asking for the floating soap called Ivory®. They then maintained manufacturing methods which kept Ivory floating, and the soap soon became one of the best known products to American consumers. Today Ivory® soap is still a big seller over a hundred years later. This company continues to listen to customers by making over a million telephone interviews every year.

Being close to the customer is the way U.S. Surgical garnered 85% of a market in the billions of dollars and growing. A U.S. Surgical sales representative brought back information from a customer about early experiments with laproscopic instruments, which use small incisions for surgical procedures that are safer and less costly. Ahead of everyone else U.S. Surgical quickly developed the new instruments.

Bahco Tools of Stockholm, Sweden found out by listening to the craftsmen who used their tools that 70% of the time they used two hands on their screwdrivers. Responding to this Bahco developed a screwdriver with room for two hands which because it was so successful it led to an entire new line of tools.

Johnson Controls listens to customers. They make climate control systems for large buildings and were amazed to find out from customers that price was less important to them than ease of repair. Repairs were difficult and took too long, so Johnson developed a pull out plastic module that a building manager could pull out and replace without needing any tools. This new system was called "Metasys" and although it cost more it is sold extremely well because it was easier to install and cheaper to maintain. While Johnson's customers did not specifically ask for this product, it is the job of the company to perform a needs analysis of their customers and satisfy the customers with their innovations.

Harvard Business School professors Leonard and Rayport refer to what they call "empathic design" by observing customers or users to find ideas. This involves observing a variety of users, even video recording them. Find a variety of users, such as: those in a hurry, disabled users, high creatives, impatient people, or those using or over using the product or service for something other than intended. People have used dishwashers for an amazing array of uses including thawing frozen turkeys or boiling eggs. Observe users with a Plan or objective in mind to increase the amount of ideas.

A book called *The Virtual Corporation* by Davidow and Malone describes a corporation that listens to their customer virtually every minute. They literally give the customer exactly what they want right at the moment. The product (or service) is created to the customer's exact wishes, which brings listening to the customer to a new dimension where the customer literally controls the corporate process. Toshiba had a slogan in 1985, "synchronize production in proportion to customer demand." 7-Eleven Japan Inc. monitors each sale to the customer with an exotic multi million dollar computer system, and can respond almost instantly with products to the shelf. This flexibility is paying off and they now have 12,925 locations in Japan (2010).

John Sealy Brown, was a V.P. and director of Xerox's R & D facility at Palo Alto, California research Center (PARC). Today he is a speaker and writer and calls himself "Chief of Confusion." He talks about co-producing with the customer. He means more here than just answering customers needs; rather, he means to probe and elicit hidden needs which can then be satisfied by the corporation. Listen to customers: one on one, through consumer research groups, in customer seminars, though social media, during new product introduction, by informal survey, with computer tracking, and through complaints or suggestions received. Also listen to employees who are sometimes users and customers too.

All though you are listening to customers you must still be anticipating their needs using constant analysis and discussion with your team. You must also keep things in context and use your judgment. Ford asked customers what shapes they liked and they answered "ovals." So when Ford came out with a redesigned Taurus it had ovals everywhere, but looked ridiculous. No one had correctly integrated this in to the overall design.

Visualize and conceptualize in terms of consequences and effects. Consequence listening means taking the responses of customers (verbal or actions) and from that information freely extrapolate to find new ideas. Listening to customers and responding means maximum flexibility allowing you to "spin on a dime" and go in any direction necessary to satisfy market demands, and has also been called lean production (MIT study of the car industry), or agile production. This is a revolutionary feature in business, and the innovative corporation.

IBM is seeking radical business ideas from customers, stakeholders, and venture capitalists in what they refer to as EBO's (emerging business opportunities). They set up an internal entrepreneurial activity developing the business idea and have had great success, creating businesses with over $1 billion in sales (including Digital Media, and Life Sciences).

USE IMAGERY AND SYMBOLISM

A picture is worth ten thousand words.
~ Confucius (551 – 479 B.C.)

If you have to ask what it symbolizes, it didn't.
~ Roger Ebert, movie critic

The CEO and top management should use psychological communication by making symbolic acts such as personally handing out an award to an employee, taking personal interest in an employee's idea, talking about innovation, or anything that symbolizes a desire to innovate. Using symbolism is a highly effective and powerful way to communicate. During World War II a Belgian director of the French BBC suggested the "V" for victory symbol using two fingers spread apart. British Prime Minister Winston Churchill quickly adopted this symbolic communication and used it to great effect creating a powerful psychological focus on victory.

Some executives from IBM decided to start their own company and called it Lexmark International. In order to symbolize a complete break with the old rigid bureaucracy of Old Blue, they had a copy of the IBM manual placed in the middle of the factory floor encased in Lucite! When Bill Arnold was president of the Centennial Medical Center in Nashville, Tennessee and wanted increased communication he literally door his office door off its hinges, and then hung it in the ceiling of the lobby, emphasizing his open door policy!

When Nicolas Hayek introduced the swatch fashion watches instead of spending large amounts of money on advertising, he used a symbol; a 13 ton, 500 foot high, working watch placed next to the tallest skyscraper in Frankfurt, Germany. Such a bold symbol communicates the company's believe that they have something great. They also did this on the Ginza in Tokyo for the Japanese introduction. This symbolic statement made a powerful introduction for the product, and also created a lot of positive feelings at the company.

When Jack Welch was a group executive at General Electric he would personally send a thank you note to a purchasing person who found a way to save some money.

Psychologist Warren Bennis did a survey of top leaders to determine features of their personality. The most commonly shared feature was having a compelling vision about their work. I believe a company must have this same compelling vision and it must be described in imagery and symbolism. The ambiguity of imagery and symbolism allows the consumer to see whatever values are meaningful to them personally, and therefore becomes highly efficient marketing. There should be both a visually and verbally stimulating environment. New imagery can create new meaning for old concepts. AT&T created a new symbol after the break up of Bell Telephone. This symbol is a stylistic representation of the earth, and implies a global vision.

The ambiguity of imagery and symbolism allows for another feature of psychological creativity. Ambiguity allows for freer thought association and free extrapolation in the mind's eye. In the article *The Mind's Eye: Nonverbal Thought in Technology (Science)* Eugene S. Ferguson makes a strong argument for the importance of imagination in invention and creativity. Imagery and symbolism gives meaning to the company's vision and helps describe for the employees in an ambiguous way how that vision is pursued. This ambiguity allows for the employee to apply themselves toward the company's vision adding their own creativity to the company's goals. Symbolism also enhances and elaborates the vision.

In marketing you can use innovative symbolism to define your product or service in a new way. For example, years ago Perrier sparkling water was presented with a twist of lemon and shown as a sophisticated drink, appealing to a group desiring something more exotic to drink at a restaurant than just a glass of water, and consequently they expanded their customer base. Using symbolism, you can define your product or service in the market in many innovative and different ways such as; something for athletes, youth oriented, the best available, for single people, for people in a hurry, the easiest to use, or other ways, and develop and own the niche.

USE FACILITATORS

The new leader is a facilitator, not an order giver.
    ~ John Naisbitt, futurist author

Shakespeare wrote in *Hamlet* of the "thousand natural shocks flesh is heir to." Change is a destructive process and the shock related to change can cause non-cooperation, power struggles, emotional difficulties and a failure to adapt. The facilitator's job goes two ways; one is to facilitate the innovator and the other is to facilitate the acceptance of the innovation by others. Niccolo` Machiavelli (1469 to 1527) wrote in his book *The Prince*, "There is nothing more difficult to take in hand, more perilous to conduct, than to take a lead in the introduction of a new order of things, because the innovation has for enemies all those who have done well under the old conditions and lukewarm defenders in those who may do will under the new." The facilitator is the oil that greases the wheel of innovation.

At Toyota they have a "Shusa" who is a supercraftsman acting as a facilitator, and at Honda they have what they call a Large Project Leader or "LPL." At BP America, a Ohio based subsidiary of British Petroleum, they are so serious about innovation they have created a special facilitator for it; this executive title is "Vice-President, Change." Des Curran is the "Ambassador for Innovation " at the innovative company 3M. At USAA banking and insurance Mick Simonelli has the title of "Enterprise Innovation Executive Leader." These companies are among a group of companies where a facilitator for innovation has become a specific job description with a specific job title! At the Hallmark Cards Company they used to have a facilitator called the "Creative Paradox." This person acted as a go between the upper management and the people on the line. Additionally, the "Creative Paradox" gave training classes in psychological creativity. Other companies thought highly of Hallmark's "Creative Paradox." Companies such as Apple Computers, Quaker Foods, and NCR, have all hired him to give training on creativity. Studies show that training for creativity increases creative ability.

At Xerox, a company always on the leading edge of innovation, they have a innovation facilitator known as an "Ombudsman."

This person controls funds which they can allocate to fund any interesting ideas employees create. The General Motors project coordinator for the creation of the Pontiac Fiero was Hulki Aldikacti. The title he came up with for a facilitator was "Team Communicator." This person smoothed the flow of ideas between members of the groups. It is significant that the Fiero project was brought to market two years earlier than the normal General Motors process.

In a Business week article Hewlett Packard V.P. of research Joel Birnbaum called previous head of research Frank Carrubba (now with Phillips) an "agent for change." There can be regular meetings with facilitators in order that the facilitator might draw out and elicit ideas. Employees must be encouraged to verbalize their ideas, in order to elaborate and draw from the subconscious. The facilitator acts as a "sounding board." Well thought out questionnaires can be used to probe suggestions and find underlying concepts and needs. Facilitators can organize technical forums, discussion groups, and sessions on creativity. They can coordinate the interaction of groups. Several facilitators can work together as an idea review board like they have at IBM where every idea is reviewed.

Although creativity and innovation is characterized by loose unorganized activity, you must have some kind of formal innovation structure in place, with all ideas in the business unit funneling into a single review. Develop a system that assures all ideas are systematically reviewed.

USE POSITIVE VERBAL REINFORCEMENT

Killer idea! ~ Anonymous

One of the most convenient and easy to use verbal reinforcements can be represented by the acronym PATS; pleases and thank yous. The anthropologist Margaret Mead called this "the oil that lubricates society." While positive reinforcement (B. F. Skinner) has a relatively weak effect compared to negative reinforcement, it has a very long range effect in time, and therefore can change behavior permanently if applied continuously, consistently, and systematically for a cumulative effect. (Negative reinforcement is initially powerful but has a temporary effect. It is followed with compensatory behavior, and is not instructive).

Some of the positive phrases that can be used to reinforce behavior that leads to innovation:
1. "That's really different."
2. "That's a wild idea."
3. "I've never heard of anything like that before."
4. "It's nice to see something new."
5. "I think you should take that idea even further."
6. "That's some unique thinking."

7. "I never heard such a good idea."

8. "You've out done your self."

9. "Every one will like that idea."

10. "I wish I had thought of that."

Positive verbal reinforcement is the only psychology to have been used for positive bottom line benefit at companies such as Emery Freight, 3M, and Weyerhauser Lumber. Studies done by these companies showed increased performance by using positive verbal reinforcement. Keep in mind the reinforcement should occur closely in time to the behavior event and should be applied in a consistent manner.

MENTOR/PROTEGE SYSTEM

The mind is not a vessel to be filled, but a fire to be kindled.
   ~ Plutarch (c.46 to 120 A.D.)

In learning you will teach, and in teaching you will learn.
   ~ Phil Collins, musician

In the 8th century B.C. Homer first introduced the mentoring concept in his Greek epic poem *The Odyssey*. Before he leaves on his journeys, Ulysses asks his servant Mentor to assist Ulysses son in learning "every facet of life." Mentoring is a long proven and respected process. Gifford Pinchot III relates in his book

Intrapreneuring how Michael Phillips was helped by Bob Dewey when Master Card was starting. Mr. Dewey was older and more experienced than Phillips and backed him in what he did because Phillips said "he had chosen to trust me." At 3M Art Fry had a mentor who helped clear the way for him, and at Pepsico CEO Donald Kendall had a mentor in Edward Loughlin. Kendall was a mentor to John Sculley who later went on to Apple computers.

Generally, mentors are someone who guides some less experienced person in a company through the corporate culture, and can give confidence to the protege because of the mentor's greater status in the company. A mentor is important for innovation because the protege will be challenging the status quo with new ideas, and the mentor's greater status adds validation to the protege's ideas. The respect, openness, and trust they develop for each other allows for this effective exchange of ideas. The mentor helps fit the ideas of the protege to the core vision of the business, and while doing this they stimulate and develop their own understanding and knowledge of every topic discussed. This system therefore also helps to develop new ideas in the mind of the mentor. At W. L. Gore & Associates (best known for their breathable, water-proof Gore-Tex®) each new employee is assigned a sponsor who is both mentor and advocate.

According to learning theory, feedback is essential to efficient thinking. The mentor acts as a "sounding board" for the protege, giving them constructive criticism and positive encouragement using positive verbal reinforcement. When the mentor guides the protege towards the goals of the company they clarify their own ideas, and also keep themselves focused on the goals of the company. Also, with the help of mentor the protege can avoid organizational barriers to new ideas. Both the mentor and the protege benefit from this system, as well as the company. Just the acceptance of the mentor concept at companies increases the communication level, as people attempt to establish relationships.

Companies such as GE have formal programs for the mentor/protege concept. At Sun Microsystems they have assigned mentors called "Sunvisors." The Nation's Business reported about a computer consulting firm, Fu Associates run by Ed Fu. Mr. Fu's word for the mentor relationship is "Fu-izing" and they have a formal but unstructured system which supports the mentor/protege process.

Mentoring is an essential technique in the innovation process and should operate continuously. Its key feature is that it is a voluntary, unstructured relationship with formal recognition within the company. The innovative company must see its employees as a valuable resource to be used to best advantage, obtaining as many ideas as possible. Great quantities of ideas must be produced to get a continuous supply of ideas, some leading only to incremental innovations, but others resulting in important breakthroughs. The company should facilitate the acquisition of ideas. Organizations such as The Mentoring Institute, a Canadian company in Sidney, British Columbia will consult on a variety of mentoring methods such as reciprocal mentoring, or group mentoring.

An early advocate of mentoring was Dr. Willis H. Carrier. He invented air conditioning and received more than 80 patents for the conditioning of air. The U.S. Patent Office issued him a patent in 1906 titled "Apparatus for Treating Air" and in 1939 he invented the first system for the air conditioning of skyscraper office buildings. Undoubtedly, his advocacy of mentoring helped obtain the ideas necessary to make the Carrier Corporation (now a part of United Technologies) one of the most successful companies in the world today.

CROSS FERTILIZATION OF IDEAS

Share your knowledge. It is a way to achieve immortality.
    ~ Dalai Lama XIV

Lockheed Aircraft's legendary designer Kelly Johnson led the so called "skunk works" research and development team that created amazing planes like the SR-71 Blackbird and the F-117 Stealth fighter. Kelly always insisted designers and mechanics work side by side, reworking ideas to a better solution. Desks were crammed on top of one another, and some people said they even grew to like it. Some companies have gone even beyond this and are sharing work spaces with other companies. The very diversity offers a cross fertilization that is creating good ideas. Some older companies like the sense of passion from a start-up that rubs off on their people, and occasional find new hires for their business. Cross-fertilization of ideas offers an exchange of knowledge that results in new perspective and general psychological stimulation.

Bob Buckman is CEO of Buckman Laboratories, a specialty chemicals company that operates worldwide. He believes "the most powerful people in the future of Buckman Labs will be those anywhere who do the best job of transferring knowledge to others." This allows maximum use of information and gives different perspective to the same facts. During the exchange of the information there is a stimulating effect beneficial to the creation of spontaneous new ideas.

The *Houston Chronicle* once reported about new architecture at Texas Products Pipeline which was specifically designed to promote creativity and innovation according to company spokesman John Barnett. Many offices had no walls or glass walls and there was a spiral staircase connecting three floors to encourage interaction between employees. Different functional areas in the company were grouped together in what they call "neighborhoods" when working on a project. Apple Computers,

Intel, and Google all use many open work areas in order to encourage the spontaneous exchange of ideas.

Allow people to make casual visits to other areas in the business for increased communication which is usually more spontaneous and conducive to creative thinking. Have a real "open door" policy where it is a accepted part of the corporate culture that people can wander around into any area of the business, even into meetings that are being held, and freely interact. Even allow people who are not in marketing or sales, such as a line supervisor, interact with customers. Sam Walton of Walmart placed people in the corporate offices out in the stores for a week every year. Once Walton had the President of the company and the Chief Operations Officer swap positions! Walton himself was often found out at the stores and was known to show up at a loading dock at 5 AM with a box of donuts.

Genetech and Sun Microsystems and a lot of other companies have been known to have a lot of Friday night get together which included the CEO, beer, and a high degree of intellectual interaction. Duane Hartley, the General Manager of Hewlett-Packard's microwave instruments division, announced the first division beer bust with the amusing comment "the beer should get there 'just in time'" referring to the just-in-time supply concept now popular. Another way to share ideas are regular monthly luncheon meetings made up of 13 or 14 people chosen by their peers in the company. Other ways to have increased communication include technical forums (3M does this and also has the Carlton Society made up of their best scientists), guest speakers (good ones are easier to find than you think), meeting groups, quality circles, and computer E-mail. Previous Intel CEO Andrew Grove told *Fortune* that because of the rapid growth of E-mail at Intel they would be paralyzed without the 300,000 messages a day. These higher levels of information dispersion are part of the fuel that feeds innovation. LAN's and inter-department networking are vital for the high levels of information needed for efficient innovation. The information exchange available with networking in a sense puts everyone into one big room just like a Honda executive who wanted to figuratively put everyone in the company into one big room. Bigger than that, is the Internet that is the cyberspace world of author William Gibson (he originated the term "cyberspace"). Companies have rapidly signed on to the Internet which is the autonomously connected system of computers facilitated in 1991 by Timothy-Berners-Lee using hypertext transfer protocol, and has continuously grown for years reaching 2 billion users world wide by 2011. Social mediums such as Facebook and Twitter also offer new types of interconnectedness and your company must have a professional presence on these media.

Conoco CEO Constantine Nicandros said they connected hundreds of computer users in their company, knowing the increased spread of information had risks, they still preferred the benefit in increased communication and creativity. General Motors is linked by satellite to their car dealers, GMAC credit, their parts plants, distribution centers, GM factories, and zone offices. Often cited by business analysts as one of the reasons for the success of Walmart is their sophisticated interconnection of computers, including connecting to suppliers.

While sharing ideas and technology with your direct competition sounds like a radical idea, it's what Sun Microsystems did with the open computing system, Apple and IBM have joint projects, and today all the American car companies own percentages of foreign car companies and have high levels of interaction. The computer Internet also offers increased communication with the competition and the users. Even being in the same area such as the computer companies in Silicon Valley in California offers the benefits of cross fertilization of ideas.

CEO of Schlumberger Euan Baird declared in a 1999 speech titled *Innovation, Anywhere, Anytime* that there was a "revolution...bringing us a new industrial era characterized by shared knowledge."

Chapter 2 - Notes:

CHAPTER 3: NEW THINKING

FOCUSED/UNFOCUSED

I don't know how to run a newspaper, Mr. Thatcher, I just try everything I can think.

~ Orson Welles in the movie *Citizen Kane*

It's been called "directed autonomy" by Robert Waterman in his book *The Renewal Factor*. Tom Peters calls it a "tight/loose property" in his writings. Arthur Koestler referred to the Roman god Janus, a two faced god, which looked both outward and inward. All of these men are talking about a situation where people were focused on some ultimate goal but were looking inward for creativity to lead them to that goal. The goal is defined and specific but the method for getting there is left to the individual. There is autonomy on the part of the individual and in the ways they proceed toward the goal. The company has described a tightly defined description of its objectives but has remained loose in describing the criteria used to reach the goal. The institution is focused on its goal with an unfocused method for obtaining that end.

The composition of this organized anarchy is converging lines of activity which are moving together toward the goals of the company while allowing for high levels of creativity in its employees. It also means when assignments are given they should leave large amounts of leeway in the description of the job. U.S. General George Patton said "Never tell people how to do things. Tell them what to do and they will surprise you with their ingenuity." Employees can be given a vague request to "improve things in this area," allowing them to best use their own talents and professional connections to get the job done. Often, employees are far more successful than the employer had in mind, just because they were not limited in their instructions. This person knows the core beliefs of the company and will be moving in that direction. How to get there is usually best determined by employees. Harvard Business School professor Rosabeth Moss Kanter found a statistically significant relationship between innovative companies and innovations started by individual employees (*The Change Masters*). This concept of freedom in the work practices of the individual worker is related to the functioning of the free market or free competition. Freedom to satisfy the goals of the company (the demands of a free market) however the worker chooses, produces better solutions. Things such as steering committees or funding committees allows management to still have control over the direction of the company. Once again as previously stated in another section, it is extremely important that the leadership in the company is communicating the company vision and the desire to be innovative in order that the employees know where to go and have the freedom to go there. The management stays focused on the goals of the company but is unfocused in the details. This allows for maximum flexibility which allows for spontaneous creative action.

OPENNESS TO CHANGE

The past is but the beginning of a beginning, and all that is and has been is but the twilight of the dawn. ~ H.G. Wells

Things do not change; we change. ~ Henry David Thoreau

He that will not apply new remedies must expect new evils, for time is the greatest innovator.
 ~ Francis Bacon (1561 – 1626) English philosopher

The art of progress is to preserve order amid change and to preserve change amid order. ~ Alfred North Whitehead

Being open to change means being flexible while pursuing new ideas. Once an innovation is developed, a period of stability should follow. Openness to change does not mean chaos should exist constantly and in every way. Even Chaos Theory suggests stability and order due to the "strange attractors." Originally described by Poincare` in 1890, the concept was later studied (1963) by meteorologist Edward Lorenz, a professor at M.I.T. until his death in 2008 at age 90. When Lorenz was about to present a scientific paper about Chaos Theory with no title, someone suggested *Does the flap of a butterfly's wings in Brazil, set off a tornado in Texas?* Chaos Theory is about an existing underlying order to all reality, and the acutely critical importance of initial conditions. The most common example of a strange attractor in action is what happens as a marble chaotically moves and roles about a large bowl while being attracted to a final state of rest at the bottom of the bowl.

Postulate: innovation is a Chaos Theory "strange attractor" towards which chaotic economic activity inextricably moves.

Following a period of R & D which creates an innovation, that is, a potentially successful product or service, there should follow a period where that innovation is used and the business reaps the benefit of its investment. Then using good reason there should be spontaneous improvements as they're realized. Within the basic framework of innovation a policy of continuous incremental improvement should follow. Incremental innovation has been described as "rapidly inching forward." In a study of innovation in scientific instruments by Eric Von Hippel at M.I.T., minor incremental improvements were the area where business was most successful. This idea of minor incremental improvement has been used proficiently by the Japanese as previously mentioned. Any continuous incremental innovation eventually realizes a very different product or service with many small advantages over the original idea. Because of the importance of this type of innovation, a very high level of openness to change must exist because of the frequency of change and yet still "preserve order amid change." This paradox of order with change can be successful dealt with by taking it one step at a time.

Change is at the very least conceptually destructive. Many aspects of culture such as routines, relationships, beliefs, and systems may individually change or totally change. William Shakespeare wrote about "the thousand natural shocks that flesh is heir to." The shock of change and the inefficiency that happens with this shock, can be overcome by preparation. Planning and preparation for change should include a clear, concise explanation to all persons involved, relating details and the reason behind the change, and be given as soon as possible before the change. Everyone should be told how they fit into the overall picture. If this preparation is made, it will go a long way in overcoming any resistance and additionally will help eliminate misunderstanding. Leaders should tactfully deal with the inertial resistance of the corporate culture by manipulating factors that facilitate/overcome resistance, including: loss of prestige/gain in prestige, loss/gains in responsibility, loss/gains in involvement, and any other idea that will help "smooth the way" for innovation. Change can cause stress and psychologists even rate the levels of stress. Stress associated with change can be harmful or healthy depending on how the person deals with it. This is also true of corporations.

With the proper preparation the company can thrive on change and be prepared to deal with changes in the future. Change must be considered the normal state of things and the institution should constantly be adapting. The basic instruction for change follows the company's goals for the future using the company's core beliefs but without specific instructions about how the employee should accomplish these goals. At various aspects of change, each development reaches a plateau where the benefits of the innovation is reached and put into practice and used by the company.

Openness to change includes preparation, instruction, facilitating policy, written and verbal communications, funding, and rewards. Written and verbal communication includes the use of words and phrases such as; new concepts, alteration, diversification, variation, modification, transformation, revolution, shift the scene, turn over a new leaf, and work a change.

When to change, how to change, where to change; using all the available information, a decision is made. Strongly related to psychological creativity is how people perceive reality. Changing things gives people a new perspective about what they're doing. If they do things the same way all the time they develop "tunnel vision" or "horse blinders" or their thinking gets "in a rut" and generally they resist change. It is therefore good to "force change" once in a while. Previous head of IBM, John Akers, used reorganization to stimulate new perspectives, "we reorganize for good business reasons. One of the good reasons is that we haven't reorganized in a while." Akers forced change in order to get a new perspective. When do we force these changes? There seems to be some limit to what is sensible about changing things. Akers said once "in a while" presumably when it feels right. Peter Drucker says in *Frontiers of Management* that every three years every idea in the company should be analyzed and put "on trial for its life." If what you are doing is not working absolutely perfectly then there is room for improvement. Change it. Napoleon said a general must change strategies every ten years so that he may continue winning. Peter Drucker says change every three years. Alvin Toffler in *Power Shift* says the world is divided into "the fast and the slow." Shakespeare said "The Time is ripe" for change.

Knowledge changes at a dramatic rate and the rate is increasing. Moore's Law said the number of transistors on a computer chip would double every two years, a prediction made by Intel co-founder Gordon Moore in 1965 and still holding true. Futurist, author, inventor and Director of Engineering at Google, Ray Kurzweil refers to his Law of Accelerating Returns (or LOAR). The forecast? Expect more change in the future and become an expert at living with it, working with it, and benefiting from it.

At Walmart, founder Sam Walton required employees at the

corporate headquarters to work once a year in something other than their regular positions. It was his way to force people to take a new perspective. Sam Walton was quoted in *Financial News* "We are willing to change, ... We have been very flexible and have been looking every day for changes that need to be made. But change, and the willingness to change, try anything, try anyone's idea; it might not work, but it won't break the company when it doesn't."

The idea that the concept of change (instead of stability) was the basis of economics was asserted by the American economist Joseph Schumpeter (1883-1950, overshadowed by his contemporary John Maynard Keynes) in his book *Capitalism, Socialism, and Democracy* he writes "it is competition from the new commodity, the new technology, the new source of supply, the new type of organization which commands a decisive cost or quality advantage and which strikes not at the margins of the profits and the outputs of the existing firms but at their foundations and their very lives." Schumpeter coined the phrase "creative destruction." Friedrich Hayek shared a 1974 Nobel Prize for economics and also promoted change and destruction of the status quo.

In 1926 Mark Sullivan wrote in *Our Times (Vol. I)* "Intellectual freedom and curiosity about the new, the instinct of the American mind to look into, examine, and experiment - this led to, among other things, a willingness to 'scrap' not only old machinery but old formulas, old ideas; and brought about, among other results, the condition expressed in the saying that 'American mechanical progress could be measured by the size of its scrap heaps.'"

Obviously the fuel of change has become more powerful with the advent of the computer. The other fuel of change is the increasing awareness about psychological creativity and innovation culture in business. As we become more effective as individuals in creating new ideas, and as companies become more effective at facilitating innovation, we will still see higher and higher levels of change. In the early '70's General Motors refused to accept the changes that were happening in the automobile industry. Like ostriches hiding their collective heads in the ground, GM executives road to work in nearly new cars that had been especially checked over for any problems. While hometown patriotism kept relatively high levels of "Detroit Steel" driving around Detroit, the upper management people ignored the hard cold facts of creeping upward percentages of foreign car ownership in places like Hawaii and California. Change was definitely happening and the automobile industry failed to accept this fact to the great detriment of many people's jobs, and their families, and their lives. Today the hard facts for the U.S. Postal Service is the emergence of the fax machine and e-mail that can do in mere seconds or minutes what they take over night or much longer to do. One of the greatest mistakes by companies has been to resist basic fundamental change. When refrigerated ice became available, some companies that cut and stored ice from frozen lakes worked feverishly to become more efficient. They built miles of transport ramps from the lake to the storage house. Needless to say, this did not work, nor did effective improvements made to gas lamps help compete with the electric light bulb.

Very often, people's reaction to change is that they can ignore it, overlook it, or even stop it. They can not. To paraphrase Huxley, if we do not face the facts, they can slay the mightiest of the mighty. The winning thought is if we do accept change, we can overcome any difficulties one day at a time, by using planning and by applying our creativity and intelligence.

RISK TAKING

Reasonable men adapt themselves to their environment; unreasonable men try to adapt their environment to themselves. Thus, all progress is the result of unreasonable men.
    ~ George Bernard Shaw

An idea that is not dangerous is unworthy of being called an idea at all. ~ Oscar Wilde

A man's errors are his portals of discovery.
   ~ James Joyce, author

Fortune sides with him who dares.
   ~ Virgil, Roman Poet (70-19 B.C.) from *Aeneid*

As the chief executive of Matsushita (Panasonic) from 1977 to 1986, Toshihiko Yamashita said his job was to "make decisions," because if at least a decision is made a mistake can be spotted and corrected. This is a better system than missing opportunity. In the late 70's Yamashita made a bold decision to promise RCA a 4 hour video cassette recorder (VCR) (VHS) system to combat the Sony Betamax system. Zenith was backing Sony and Yamashita had to promise RCA 4 hours recording time to match the Betamax's 4 hour capability and get a contract with RCA. At the time Panasonic did not even have a design for a 4 hour recorder, and was taking a great risk. However, the risk paid off and Panasonic won a great part of a billion dollar market.

Ross Johnson, head of RJR Nabisco said he was usually going with "gut feel decisions with limited market research" in developing new products. Although this seems very risky, decisions sometimes need to be made following one's hunches or instincts, and anecdotal evidence recalls the likes of American greats such as J.P. Morgan and Cornelius Vanderbilt. The New Jersey Institute of Technology studied precognition in CEO's; E.

Douglas Dean, a parapsychologist, found that 80% of CEO's who had doubled profits in 5 years had statistically significant, higher than average levels of precognitive ability. Joel S. Birnbaum, V.P. of research at Hewlett Packard told *Business Week* how Frank Carrubba, the previous head of research, had "very good intuition for which technologies will in the end workout." One very basic feature of psychological creativity is gathering information. Nabisco's Ross Johnson is surely getting more information than he thinks. An intelligent assessment of facts is being constantly processed into the subconscious and after some consideration (called incubation) he reaches his gut level decision.

It is an inherent feature of new ideas that they have many unknown features and therefore unknown risks are a part of any new idea. General George Patton told his son in a letter "take calculated risks." Risk applied on a regular basis implies failure at some point. Federal Express risked much with Zap mail but lost. The overview is that the rewards of risk taking for new ideas outweighs the negative side of concomitant failure. Failure itself has its positive side if lessons are learned and applied to future events. There is a story about IBM where an employee had just blown a project that cost about 10 million dollars. When he was called into the boss' office he thought he was going to be fired, but he was told that wasn't going to happen because they just invested $10 million in his education! At Toro, the mower manufacturer, some engineers designed a mold to make hoods on mowers. The molds didn't work well though at high volume production levels and Toro wound up losing a years worth of mower sales. When the engineers were called to the office of CEO Kendrick Melrose they thought for sure they were going to be fired. Instead Melrose had balloons and cake for them to celebrate their risk taking. Later on their molds were used successfully on some other products. *Fortune* magazine in the February 1993 issue quoted the much admired CEO of Intel Andrew Grove admitting that risk taking had cost Intel between $30 and $40 million in killed projects during the last 6 months. Risk taking is consequently a learning process. From Yamashita's perspective, risk taking is a win/win process which is infinitely better than no decision at all.

Mike Markkula at Apple Computer said in the book *Leadership Challenge* by Kouzes and Posner "The overall quality of work improves when you give people a chance to fail." This chance to fail is the mechanism that allows the greater reaches of risk taking and the learning process of failure. Eric Hoffer wrote in *The Ordeal of Change* "There can be no real freedom without the freedom to fail." At the University of Houston Jack Matson had a class that was known as "failure 101." Students competed to build very tall structures out of ice cream sticks and were advised by Matson to find "insight in every failure." Those who had the most failures always won. Disney CEO Michael Eisner said he wanted Disney to be a place "in which people feel safe to fail."

Risk taking can define limits and the re-conceptualization following failure can lead to success.

Taking a risk is an integral part of any life process. Taking a risk on something will not cause your company to fail (remember Sam Walton) as long as you use good sense in deciding when to let an idea go. Just trying something, anything might bring some valuable result. An old Persian fairy tale tells the story of the Three Princes of Serendip. Without any particular goal in mind the princes sailed about the world aimlessly. They risked these dangerous voyages and always seemed to find ideas and things of value to take back home. The word serendipity is derived from these Princes of Serendip. Rosabeth Moss Kanter relates in *The Change Masters* the second most important feature of innovative companies in her study was a willingness to take risks of every kind (collaborative managers was first). Conceptual, financial, personal, professional, and risks of time.

Risk taking should always involve some level of rational thinking and assessment of the idea in combination with intuitive reasoning, a "calculated risk." Chrysler feared risking on something as simply as a child's car seat to better protect children, a seemingly good idea. Employee Ron Zarowitz had an idea for a built in car seat for children but it took Chrysler 6 years to warm up to the idea. When finally added as a $200 option it sold like hotcakes and they realized they had lost years of profits. The greater the risks the greater the rewards. Remember, the great Babe Ruth lead the major leagues in strike outs as well as home runs. The Babe just took more chances!

ALLOW RULE BREAKING THINKING

'Speak when you're spoken to!' The Queen sharply interrupted her. 'But if everybody obeyed that rule,' said Alice, who was always ready for a little argument, 'and if you only spoke when you were spoken to, and the other person always waited for you to begin, you see nobody would ever say anything, so that ...' 'Ridiculous!' cried the Queen.
~ Lewis Carroll, *Alice in Wonderland*

At Ford a new system was put into place to build the first Taurus. This way of building cars broke all the rules. The Taurus went on to become the most profitable car in automotive history. Traditionally, manufacturing started with a vague idea from the upper levels of management about what kind of car they wanted. This idea was given to design, then engineering, then manufacturing, then suppliers, then sales, and then the customer was the last one to find out what the car was about. Throughout this process accountants were continuously forcing every thing to be done as cheaply as possible and consequently sometimes inadequately. They broke all the rules with their new process, which is known as simultaneous engineering. This technique combines all the other processes into just one process. Everything is done at the same time with a constant feedback between members. This immediate feedback process is much more efficient and a lot faster which means saving large sums of money. Simultaneous engineering means the process has become more of an art form, like a sculptor chipping away at a rock, constantly getting feedback about the state of the design, every moment reconsidering his direction. More creativity is put into this process and more consideration of many people's ideas goes into the process. Even customers were included in the process up front instead of being the last to be allowed to give their opinion. On the Taurus, customers said they had a hard time finding the seat adjustment which was down there Somewhere under the seat. The final design was a bar that transverses the entire bottom of the seat front. Normally, this bar which cost about a dollar more would have been denied by the cost cutting accountants. After all, a dollar on a million cars is one million dollars, a lot of money. Peter Drucker has written about needing a new cost accountancy for innovation, and on the Taurus they did it. They decided to place the needs of the consumer above cost cutting. Engineering people at Ford could design the car to be as strong as a tank but after listening to people with a different perspective they realized they were over building some things at great expense. Also, manufacturing asked for a grab hold piece to be placed in the design so that some part like a door could be moved with less resulting damage. Ford also started using suppliers in the process up front, with the same improvements as with manufacturing. These kind of interactions lead to a much higher quality car and a highly profitably car company. Simultaneous engineering is a revolutionary process.

Tom Watson Jr. head of IBM used to tell a story about wild ducks flying south. A kind person started putting out feed on a nearby pond and instead of flying south, some of the wild ducks stayed on. Soon these ducks grew fat and lazy living off the feed and did not even fly any more. So Watson would make the point that you can make wild ducks tame but you can't make tame ducks wild. He felt it important that IBM needed a few wild ducks (unique thinkers) so as not to fall into a dangerous conformity. On the original IBM 360 computer scientists were told specifically to abandon a particular line of research, which they secretly continued until they succeeded.

At 3M an employee was told to abandon a project and when he refused he was ultimately fired. Even though this person was not even suppose to be on the premises, they took over an abandoned office and continued working on the project, eventually becoming successful and re-hired. Rules can be guidelines that tell people they should be very sure if they vary beyond this point. However, there should be some ambiguous overreach beyond rules that allows for the creativity of the individual. A psychology or creation that is unique can not be predicted by rules, and is accommodated by a tolerance for rule breaking.

When employees have a profound sense about the need to do something beneficial for the company, they have broken the rules in many ways, such as taking money from one budget and putting it into another, using advertising money to develop a product, paying people more than company policy, or instituting services to customers without any upper approval.

RELINQUISH CONTROL

Most of what we call management consists of making it difficult for people to get their work done. ~ Peter Drucker

If everything seems under control, you're just not going fast enough. ~ Mario Andretti, American Race Car Driver

Peter Drucker makes a sweeping statement in the opening paragraph of his book *Innovation & Entrepreneurship*. He believes American business has moved from a managerial to an entrepreneurial style. That is, he is referring to what is popularly being called empowerment. Basically, this means giving responsibility to the employee, allowing an employee to act something like an entrepreneur. This is a critically important perspective allowing for an organization that responds to a "free market" in all its individual parts and also allows for the ambiguity that produces creative thinking and innovation.

One of the side benefits of empowering employees is an increase in their motivation to work (as shown in a study at Averitt Express the trucking company). Greater rewards (more powerful reinforcement) are created when a person makes a decision of their own free will and based on their own intelligence. This system of empowerment also is more effective in the case of negative reinforcement; the employee will more quickly desert an unsuccessful idea when it has become overwhelmingly obvious the idea is a failure. This sense of failure may be tapping an intuitive understanding of the situation which is absent in bureaucratic policy. NCR is an example where a successful company pursued a policy that was unsuccessful. They continued to invest in and build electro-mechanical calculators at a time when an individual's intuition might have told them that the electronic calculator would soon over whelm the market. NCR lost millions of dollars.

CEO Jack Welch of multi billion dollar G.E. told *Fortune* magazine (1991) "we've got to take out the Boss element." Welch was determined to make his giant company a creator of ideas by empowering his employees. Because the Hughes Laboratories empowered Dr. Theodore Maiman to follow his own intuition, the LASER was created in 1960. American business leader H. Ross Perot (previous GM board member) speaks in down to earth terms when he describes the inefficiency of the old industrial corporate model of decision making; " At GM, if you see a snake, the first thing you do is go hire a consultant on snakes, and then you discuss it for a couple of years. The most likely course of action is nothing. You figure, the snake hasn't bitten anybody yet, so you just let him crawl around on the factory floor... I come from an environment where, the first guy who sees the snake kills it." (*Perot* by Todd Mason).

In recent years companies like Apple Computers, Cummins Diesel, Frito-Lay and others have decentralized decision making by pushing authority downward to the local level. GM reorganized in 1984 into a small car group (Chevrolet and Pontiac) and a big car group (Buick, Olds, Cadillac). The purpose of this was to give an increase responsibility to the individual divisions. Successful corporations today are empowering employees.

At Intel, CEO Andrew Grove talked about people making strategy for the company with their fingertips. The actual people who are in touch with what is happening can make action specific decisions at the very moment something is happening. This allows decision making that is better coordinated with the facts. Strategy which has filtered down through the hierarchy cannot do this. This also relates to a recurring theme of the innovative corporation, that is, flexibility. Flexibility means providing answers and solutions to a greater variety of situations. 3M'rs can spend 15 % of their budgets any way they think might be beneficial. Google employees are allowed to spend up to 20% of their time on any project they feel will help the company. That's usually as much as one day a week. Companies should allow uncontrolled, spontaneous action in certain situations. When John Henderson was Director of Hallmark Card's Creative Resources Center he said "you have to build a climate and give people the freedom to create things."

Psychological spontaneity is a key feature of any company that is successful in innovation. Many companies such as Sun Microsystems, and Apple are known for their spontaneous style. Microsoft's Bill Gates said " There's a basic philosophy here that by empowering...workers you'll make their jobs far more interesting, and they'll be able to work at a higher level." Humor, playfulness, uncontrolled debate, and other spontaneous actions are elemental parts of innovation.

MEDITATION & REFLECTION

Study without reflection is a waste of time; reflection without study is dangerous.
   ~ Confucius, Chinese philosopher, (551 – 479 B.C.)

The imagination, courage, and brooding meditation of the

inventive faculty.

~ Elmer Sperry, *The Spirit of Invention in an Industrial Society*

There is a story about Henry Ford and an efficiency expert. Ford hired the man to analyze operations at Ford's auto manufacturing plant. After a complete review the so called expert came to Ford recommending several changes. His most emphatic recommendation was to get rid of the man in the office several doors down the hall from Ford. "Why?" said Mr. Ford. "Well" the expert answered "every time I go by that guy's door I see him in there with his feet up on the desk just staring into space, totally wasting your time." Ford shot back, "Leave that man alone! He's been in that exact position many times when he's saved me millions of dollars!"

While taking action is important it is obvious that it must be proceeded by thinking. One of the features of psychological creativity is altered states of consciousness that help release from the subconscious mind ideas that have formed there. Companies like Exxon have responded with recreational facilities and wooded and park like areas around the place of business for relaxation and contemplation. Some companies have provided special rooms for thinking and some have soothing sounds playing such as the ocean or the sound of a gently falling rain. Gould Pump of Seneca Falls , New York provided employees with a million dollar 21 acre recreational facility. Also use retreats, special trips of any kind, company seminars, and task forces to allow an employee to get into an new frame of mind which gives them a new perspective on business or allows for the releasing of ideas from the mind.

It is worth here to quote at length the Italian novelist Matteo Bandello describing the contemplative technique of Leonardo Da Vinci, creating one of the most recognizable works of art in all the world, the *Last Supper* (located in the Refectory of St. Maria delle Grazie.) Bandello wrote " Many a time I have seen Leonardo go to work early in the morning and climb on to the scaffolding, because the Last Supper is somewhat above ground level; and he would work there from sunrise until the dusk of evening, never laying down the brush, but continuing to paint without remembering to eat or drink. Then there would be two, three, or four days without his touching the work, yet each day he would spend one or two hours just looking, considering and examining it, criticizing the figures to himself. I have also seen him (when the caprice or whim took him) at midday when the sun is highest leave the Corte Vecchia, where he was working on the stupendous Horse of clay, and go straight to the Grazie; climbing on the scaffolding, he would pick up a brush and give one or two brushstrokes to one of the figures, and then go elsewhere."

ALIGN POLICY FOR INNOVATION

Your paints are living men and your brushes wit and cunning.
~ Niccolo` Machiavelli

The energy company Amoco (merged with BP in 1998) surveyed its employees and discovered they were not inclined to take risks in their work. Risk taking is one of the features of creativity and Amoco decided to align policy so as to accommodate risk taking by their employees. Amoco went beyond the innovative companies which allowed persons to seek alternate sponsors or support for ideas in other departments in the company (this is also allowed at 3M). Amoco created a plan which would allow company departments to participate in joint ventures with outside groups, if Amoco was unwilling to back the idea in the first place. This daring alignment of policy forced Amoco management to take a good look at any new ideas brought to them.

In a *Working Woman* magazine issue, business author Tom Peters quite eloquently stated that you do not manage human imagination, rather "you create a garden." A company's internal structure must reflect the external environment which is in constant change. That means the company must be changing and as ad hoc groups form in unique new combinations in response to the current problems they face, the company must align policy so as to coordinate and facilitate the root functioning of the company. If someone is required to go through a lengthy application period in order to get funding for a new idea, that policy itself may be hindering the fast movement of ideas into your business. Systematically examine your written and unwritten polices to assure they facilitate innovation. You should also have a basic written policy that specifically addresses and accommodates innovation.

EGALITARIAN VALUES

We hold these Truths to be sacred and undeniable; that all men are created equal.
   ~ Thomas Jefferson, *Declaration of Independence*

Promote communication and sharing of ideas, and motivate people by removing inequalities between employees. At IBM one of the main tenets of Thomas Watson Sr. was "respect for the individual." H. Ross Perot has said of his company EDS that it has "only one class of employee." Both these legendary American businessmen realize in these statements that every job is extremely important. The head of a company cannot function without its members. Each job must be performed with the highest level of efficiency, quality, and innovation, so that the overall company can be successful. At Chaparral Steel, the world's lowest-cost producer of steel, CEO Gordon Forward put forth the idea of a classless corporation as one of the reasons for his company's success. "We figured if we could tap the ego's of everyone in the company, we could move mountains." Motivated employees invented a new highly efficient mill for making beams in bridges, and developed a new, and better strapping machine for bundling steel which costs only $60,000 versus the $250,000 they were spending.

One company known for innovation was computer pioneer Digital Equipment Corporation, founded and run until 1998 by Ken Olsen (1926 - 2011). This leader of a billion dollar company was known as 'Ken' to everyone. The place of business had mostly open office spaces, very few private offices, and no dress code of any kind. Intel is another example.

A business needs motivated employees and most companies have an opportunity to be much more effective by paying attention to this fact. A person does not just "act" motivated, rather, they are motivated by something outside of themselves. They respond to the company's act of respect towards them. It is significant and important to point out that if this process of respect is clearly established, then the employee will stay motivated beyond the specific moment of respect. The person's motivation can continue into any part of the job, yet the employer should take any opportunity to move the employee to higher levels of motivation. Even superhuman achievements have been reported in the history of humankind as a result of some great motivating factor.

Mutual respect also delivers the highest levels of efficiency when working in groups. Studies show that the most effective groups learn to rely on each others strengths. When psychological barriers are removed people can work in synergistic ways which makes the group more effective than the sum of its parts.

Chapter 3 – Notes:

CHAPTER 4: RESOURCES

BUDGET MONEY FOR INNOVATION

The empires of the future are the empires of the mind.
~ Sir Winston Churchill

A study called *The Production and Application of New Industrial Technology* (New York 1977, E. Mansfield, J. Rapoport, A. Romeo, E. Villani, S. Wagner, & F. Husic) found that the return on money invested in innovation has been twice the return on money used for capital investment. Up to 1960 the company Haloid had spent 75 million dollars on the Xerox® copier concept. That year their total revenues were 60 million dollars. Just six years later (1966) their annual revenues had skyrocketed to 500 million dollars! Time, cash flow, and the ability to borrow money are the only known limits to the amount of money that can be effectively invested in innovation.

Genetech (now owned by Roche), the biotechnology company, invested 58% of sales into research and development in 1985. That was an investment of 80 million dollars in one year! In 1987 they invested 40% of revenue on R & D; 96.5 million dollars, which was an increase in dollar amount over the previous year. They invested 46.3% of sales in 1991 which was $96,698 per employee and invested $2.8 billion in 2008. Budgeting money for innovation is so important that it should be a part of your company's culture. At Bell Laboratories they refer to "the 3 F's": funding, focus, and freedom. They realize that budgeting money for innovation, having the money funded and ready for use, is a basic part of facilitating innovation. Because spontaneity is a key feature of psychological creativity, there should be funds that can move as fast as the flow of ideas. This can have significant effect at any scale. A company that needs a complete product developed before the end of the year, cannot wait until the next business quarter to arrange funding. On the scale of a short time span we again find the need for the flow of funding to match the flow of ideas. Curiosity can wane or move to another area. Many good ideas can start in the mind but then be blocked from further development by a lack of funding. In order to give the most chance to as many ideas as possible, the innovative American company 3M (formally known as Minnesota, Mining, & Manufacturing) allows 15% of budgets to be discretionary. They also have something called the "innovation bank" which is a source of funds just for new ideas at a company producing 55,000 different products and constantly changing. This allows people to spontaneously explore ideas which their intuition and senses tells them might be important. Their thinking is something unique to this person's understanding and there is little chance that upper management on corporate planning can anticipate these particular ideas. There is also a natural social inhibition in bringing a weak, fragile, underdeveloped concept and presenting it to one's superiors. Some funding as seed money gets an idea started that might not have been otherwise explored.

Allow anyone in the company to approach any funding committee with an idea. At Conoco a special committee administered a funding source called "SEED." Genetech, Sun Microsystems, 3M, and Xerox are all recognized as innovative leading edge companies. Some companies invest more time and money in developing innovations. Some have better systems in place to facilitate innovation by design, so that with the same amount of investment they stay at a higher level of innovation. In the book *The Change Masters* Rosabeth Moss Kanter studied 115 innovations from 6 companies. The more innovative companies used significantly higher amounts of resources, including money. Analysts generally predict higher growth and earnings for companies with higher R & D.

In general, business invests between 2% and 12% of revenues into research and development. The American company 3M uses 6.5% of revenue and Merck Pharmaceuticals, one of America's most admired companies invested an average of 11.5% and between 1980 and 1989 an investment of $4.5 billion in research (Business Week June 29, 1992). Ericsson has invested as much as 24.9% of revenues, while Apple has invested as little as 2.2% of revenues (2011). Microsoft spent about 17% of revenues for

R&D in 2010. Sony spent about 8% (2010). BMW and Honda spend the largest total dollar investment as a percentage of revenue in the automotive world at 5.5% (2010) however, Volkswagen's total dollar investment exceeded both Toyota and GM combined with $8 billion in 2009. In 2011 Toyota was the top spender with $9.9 Billion (4.2% of sales), second place was Novartis with $9.6 Billion (16.4% of sales), and in third place Roche Holding at $9.4 Billion (19.6% of sales; highest percentage in the top 20 companies).

Both the U.S and Japan have invested an average 3% of their Gross Domestic Product into research and development with Japan usually in second place, however increased spending in China has now moved them into second behind the United States. The high percentage spender has been Israel with 4.3% of GDP. The United States' investment must be higher though because of the amount of secret investment in military projects which must be considered because of the basic technological advances made there. Worldwide growth in spending has been averaging 7% to 8% a year. Intel has increased their R&D investment every year. The biggest spender was the U.S. with $402 billion spent in 2009. China with $154 billion, and Japan with $138 billion invested. World investment including third world nations is about one percent of GDP, so you must be investing more than one percent of sales or you are totally off the mark. However as I have indicated, innovation is somewhat an art which is crafted along the way, considering the needs of the moment, the esthetic, social, business, cultural, accommodations, skills, intuition and other resources so that no exact formula exists to tell us how to invest in innovation. Nevertheless, we must make this financial and psychological investment in the future.

There are government programs to help business develop in the area of basic research. Some examples include; the Commerce Department's Advanced Technology Program, and the Defense Department's Technology Reinvestment Program. Other sources include the National Technical Information Service, and the National Science Foundation.

CEO Alan Jacobson of 3M told *Fortune* magazine "I never want to hear anyone put down a project because it isn't in the budget." Any budget can become ineffective if it is used to make decisions with out regard to good business sense. A budget is only a guide line to keep things in perspective, and should not dictate actions in the face of changing situations and new opportunities. Management author Peter Drucker specifically states (*Harvard Business Review*) that a new business accountancy is needed for the future. Under the old system, even a simple improvement is considered a cost and cannot be justified. This type of thinking totally eliminated innovation. Therefore, Mr. Drucker calls for a new type of accountancy which integrates thinking for innovation.

After working at Ford Motors, Don Frey (vice president, product development) said " a bean counter's idea of cost control, I surmised, was to take an inch off the tail pipe every year" (*Harvard Business Review*). His statement does not condemn accountants but a form of accountancy. A new accountancy is needed which considers innovation a normal and important part of the business and a part of the budget.

REWARD INNOVATION

Keep on sowing your seed, for you never know which will grow, perhaps it all will. ~ Albert Einstein

Napoleon is said to have responded to criticism about a medal he awarded "you lead men by baubles not words!" While words and the images described by them are indeed important, the fact recognized in Napoleon's statement is that the symbolism of actions and objects is also important and effective in motivating people. They are concrete and real things and can speak more than words. Top performing companies recognize this fact. Conoco studied their reward system and discovered they were rewarding old business practices more than innovation and changed the system to emphasize innovation. Some rewards are in the work itself; a sought after assignment, personnel needed for a future job, larger amounts of funding, or greater access to information. At Apple computers a small number of employees receive the title; DEST "Distinguished Engineer/Scientist, Technologist."

Tata Group is a company in India founded in 1868 with 100 billion dollars in revenues in 2012, and clearly one of the greatest companies in India (and the world). They are involved in seven different business sectors, including ownership of Jaguar cars and the world's lowest cost car the Tata Nano at $2,500 USD. Their annual innovation awards includes one for failure called "Dare to Try" because people's natural instinct is to stop trying after failure. This can not happen at the innovative organization.

At the Toyota automobile company their most prestigious award is the "Presidential Award." This recognition for achievement is given to employees of the company. In the reserved Japanese way the award consists of a simple engraved pen; however, it is personally delivered by the head of this multi billion dollar company. This recognition is the final level in psychologist Abraham Maslow's *Hierarchy of Needs Theory,* a level which must be fulfilled before a person can "self actualize" and reach the fullness of their potential. This need in people is fulfilled by ritual, ceremony, and the symbolism this creates which makes up and describes the culture of the organization.

Some companies allow a choice of profit sharing or a bonus on specific ventures. Panasonic rewards up to one million yen for a good idea. Japanese employees receive as much as 30 % of their yearly income from bonuses tied to personal performance and how well the company performs as a whole. At IBM they pay up to 25% of accrued savings during the first 2 years of an idea. Employees sometimes make six figure bonuses from this and IBM is happy to pay it. One IBMer suggested product serial numbers be labeled instead of stamped and saved IBM 70 million dollars! At Bell Atlantic they have a "Champion Program" which gives the champion of a product 5% of the revenue (with caps) if it gets to market. Too often awards become meaningless because they are given for performance that is not really exceptional, so be sure to be making meaningful rewards for real performance.

Other awards besides money include; letters of recommendation, dinners with upper management, an elaborate permanent trophy which is passed year to year, art objects with an engraved plague, useful objects such as pens or tools with an engraved plague. Both monetary rewards and rewards of recognition can be given to quality circles or task forces or other groups. Some awards should be given by the employees and the criteria should be determined by the employees. At Tandem Computers they had a bulletin board listing what was called people's "latest and greatest." Keep in mind that employee incentive programs must be designed so that the employee considers how their performance is affecting the goals of the entire company.

AVOID STEREOTYPE HIRING

Once you label me you negate me.
 ~ Søren Kierkegaard (1813 to 1855, Danish Philosopher)

Donald E. Peterson, a previous head of Ford Motor Company, points out in his book that people in the personnel department tend to pick out a "safe hire." But if they do this all the time they will "miss opportunities to bring creative innovators into your business".

Ben Rich was the man who succeeded Kelly Johnson at Lockheed Aircraft, and the man who led the development of the incredible F-117 Stealth Fighter. In his book he states that he believes in the broad value of generalists "who are more open to unconventional approaches than narrow specialists." The first working model of a LASER was developed by Dr. Theodore Maiman at Hughes. Dr. Maiman contends that his varied background; electrical engineering, physics, optics, vacuum systems, and a PhD. thesis on a gas made him uniquely qualified for his accomplishment.

Creative innovators represent unusual points of view which forces other team members to be more flexible in their thinking. Flexibility is another feature of creativity. People from different disciplines may have existing solutions which have a parallel application to problems the company is facing. A varied experience means they will be applying different principles and tools to see new solutions.

At IBM they have deliberately created a counter culture called the IBM Fellows. These people dress any way they want and do anything else they want to do. This high degree of freedom allows them to bring any kind of thinking to the work they do. IBM once ran full page ads asking for "Dreamers, Heretics, & Gadflies" in an attempt to hire unique thinkers. Go totally outside the normal hiring process and hire outside inventors to add innovative ideas to your company. These people work on their own outside of the social pressure of peer groups at the office. Any kind or amount of social pressure can kill an idea or lead it down the wrong path. Toro is a Bloomington, Minnesota manufacturer of lawn mowers and grounds equipment. They wanted an improved aerator to use on golf courses and hired independent inventor Bob Comer for the job. The problem with the existing type was when holes were poked in the ground (to aerate) it threw up a lot of dirt and forced the closing of the golf course so they could clean up. This meant losing money for the business owning the golf course. Mr. Comer came up with the idea to use high power jets of water which just leaves a nice clean hole. It's called the Toro hydro-jet and it outsold the competition 2 to 1!

You can use the classic Miller Analogies Test (www.pearsonassessments.com) to hire people with an ability to see relationship in ambiguous situations, a feature of psychological creativity. Also, widely used in testing for creatives is the Torrance® Tests of Creative Thinking (TTCT) available at (www.ststesting.com).

EMPLOYEE TRAINING

If I have seen further it is by standing on the shoulders of giants.
  ~ Sir Isaac Newton (1642-1727)

Where observation is concerned, chance favors only the prepared mind. ~ Louis Pasteur (1822-1895)

Japan is attempting to reverse the rigid consensus model which has permeated Japanese life and business, by training for creativity. At Omron Corporation, an electronic controls manufacturer, they have a monthly "juku" where the participants attempt to obtain a new perspective and become more creative by acting as 19th century warlords or acting as private detectives. Fuji Films has their upper management people do things like studying the history of Venice or the sociology of apes. Takashi Kamiya was a human resource manager at Fuji. He realized what all companies need to understand, "you can't just tell your employees 'be creative!' you have to create an environment that caters more to the individual" in order to release the creativity of the individual.

The ABC evening news once had a story about some unusual training being taken by employees of Amdahl Computers. It was a unique program which had teams climbing in trees together, the idea being to inspire team members to work together and to take risks.

Chaparral Steel was the world's lowest-cost producer of steel, making steel at a new record low of 1.6 hours of labor per ton produced. One of CEO Gordon Forward's rules was universal education, and at any given time about 85% of the employees were taking a wide variety of classes. American Axle & Manufacturing is a tier one supplier to General Motors and many other automobile manufacturers. Their much admired CEO Dick Dauch says "we are absolutely fanatical about training and education." Between 1994 and 2000 AA&M invested $100 million in training. Triton Industries was cited by Inc. magazine as one of the best companies for employee practices. Triton, a metal stamping manufacturer, devotes 1.5% of sales for training. Companies like IBM have training sections in all their divisions. Training for innovation is as important as any other area of business, and should include training for creativity and functioning in autonomous groups. According to the U.S. Office of Technology Assessment (their budget ended by Speaker of the

House Gingrich, 1995) American companies gave new employees less than 50 hours of training. In CEO Dick Dauch's book *American Drive 1* he says American Axle & Manufacturing gives 30 to 50 hours per associate (2012). Japanese new employees receive 300 hours training in the first 6 months alone, six times as much training. At the Saturn Corporation they received 92 hours of training which included training for creativity. "Innovating" was a part of the Saturn team members' job description.

Formal training for employees is increasing, and the American Society for Training and Development offers ASTD's Certified Professional in Learning and Performance credential, offered by the ASTD Certification Institute. A common mistake is to invest in training almost exclusively for management. This must change if companies are to unleash employee's enormous creative power and psychological efficacy to help in reaching the company's goals.

One of the leaders in psychological creativity research is E. Paul Torrance, Head of Educational Psychology at the University of Georgia. Dr. Torrance has determined from extensive research that there is an improvement in creative ability after creativity training. It is a very significant improvement of between 70% and 90%. There is also a measured improvement in patent activity after training. Information like this is hard to ignore and indicates a lot of room for improvement in American companies. Companies such as Apple, Quaker Foods, NCR and about a third of American business is now training for creativity. This training should continue throughout a person's career and is available at places such as the Creative Education Foundation at www.creativitytraining.com.

BE INFORMED: MONITOR NEWS & STATISTICS

God give me strength to face a fact though it slay me.
 ~ Thomas H. Huxley, English Biologist (1825-1895)

It's a capital mistake to theorize before one has data.
 ~ Arthur Conan Doyle, *The Memoirs of Sherlock Holmes, The Crooked Man*

Dr. John Dessauer of the then named Haloid company, read an article one day in a magazine called Radio News about a copying process. He brought the idea to Haloid and it eventually became known as Xerox. They coined the term xerography which came from the Greek for "dry writing". While many other factors are responsible for the success of Xerox, it may have never happened with out Dr. Dessauer discovering that magazine article.

George Eastman read an article in an English almanac about reducing the weight and size of a camera. He then designed a small camera and gave it a name, Kodak®. It came with 100 exposures, and was returned camera and all to the factory for developing. The company became a giant of industry.

Monitor statistics such as: demographics, popular opinion, technology, new products, the workforce, and facts such as competition, hero's in the world, finance, insider newsletters, securities analysts, professional conferences, social media, and the industry you are in via trade journals and trade shows. Visit trade shows outside your industry to gain new perspective. Also research patents issued in your area but not being used. New ideas are being patented every day which your company may be able to obtain and use. These are good ideas sometimes that have not been used yet because of lack of capital or because others did not see the full potential. Chester Carlson was approaching large companies with his idea for a copying machine (eventually known as Xerox) because he didn't have the money to market it himself. Many good ideas are waiting to be rediscovered. Charles Gerhardt first discovered aspirin and produced it from the bark of the willow tree (salicylic acid). This needed to be combined with other chemicals to reduce the associated stomach pain, and Gerhardt thought the process too difficult to manufacture. Over 40 years later, Felix Hoffman successfully rediscovered it, overcame production difficulties and today over 70 million pounds of aspirin are produced yearly.

Businesses overseas occasionally have a product that can be marketed by you in your local market. Marion Laboratories (now a part of Hoechst) sold an anti-ulcer drug called Carafate with 28 million dollars in sales per year. They licensed this product from a company in Japan.

Industrial Research is an organization in New Zealand which does the research and development on many innovations that are later successful as a licensed product. One such idea developed was an acoustic tool used to measure the stiffness and fiber properties of trees. It was used later by the company Carter Holt Harvey. Stiffer logs are more valuable because it affects the wood's performance in construction. This tool allows the company to be more competitive.

When something is unexpectedly successful you should find out why. In the 1950's Ray Kroc was marketing milkshake mixers and couldn't figure out why a small drive-in in California had ordered 10 mixers for their location, more than they should have needed, so he decided to go there and look for himself. As he approached the location and saw the long lines of people, he told himself that he had "discovered something wonderful." What he discovered was the very successful Richard and Maurice McDonald Brothers' speedy and efficient burger drive-in. The brothers had thrown out complicated menus and simplified to just burgers, fries and a drink, items that were prepared and delivered immediately. Ray Kroc eventually bought out the McDonald brothers business and turned it into a chain that ultimately had thousands of locations worldwide ($27 billion in revenue in 2011 with over 34,000 locations).

MEASURE INNOVATION

In God We Trust, all others bring data. ~ W. Edwards Deming

Efficiency expert W. Edwards Deming says in his book *Out of the Crisis* that it was "statistical control that opened the way to engineering innovation and without it the process was in chaos." By measuring, engineers were able to discern a direction in which to innovate. Deming called innovation "the foundation of the future."

In *The Adaptive Corporation* (1985) Alvin Toffler describes what he calls a "novelty ratio" which is a ratio of new products to old. Peter Drucker wrote in the October '90 *Harvard Business Review* that one of the essential features for success in the future was a measurement of quality called Total Quality Management. This measurement is as vital and important in innovation as in any other area of business. You should be defining the theoretical limits of every feature of your product or service. At 3M they expect after a five year period that 25 percent of sales will be accounted for by products that didn't exist 5 years ago. At NCR

50% of sales comes from products that are 1 year old or less. At the printing company R.R. Donnelly, CEO John Walter expects 50% of revenues from new products within one year.

Fortune magazine reported about a way to measure the intellectual assets of a company developed by economist James Tobin called "Tobin's q," which is a ratio between a company's market value (stock price times shares outstanding) and the replacement value of it's physical assets. This was developed for other purposes though and is just a general indicator, but a company that is valued highly and has few physical assets is a company built of ideas. Microsoft is such a company.

The following is a list of ways innovation should be measured:
1. Time between innovations.
2. New products as a percentage of sales.
3. Research & Development money as a percentage of sales.
4. Failed new products as a percentage of sales.
5. Amount of ideas generated per employee.
6. Totals of ideas generated per year/month/week.
7. An innovation's level of originality; first of type, major, minor, incremental.
8. Ratio of ideas to successful ideas.
9. Amount of awards from outside the company.
10. Amount of recognition from the media.
11. Who, what, when, where, why, and how.

12. Ideas used as a percentage of employee suggestions.

13. Percentage of positive responses to new products/services.

14. Percentage of employees involved directly in R & D.

15. R & D as a percentage of profits.

16. R & D dollars per employee.

17. Amount of features on products or services.

EMPLOYEE CONTINUITY

A man has a right to be employed, to be trusted, to be loved, to be revered. ~ Ralph Waldo Emerson (1803-1882)

Keeping employees on the job is especially important for innovation. Job security and a stake in the company creates the social setting that is necessary for creativity. The psychologist Abraham Maslow refers to this in his *Hierarchy of Needs Personality Theory.* This theory asserts that a person must satisfy needs lower in the hierarchy such as physical needs, safety needs, and the need for belongingness before exercising the personality in the higher areas of cognitive reasoning. It is in this higher area where creativity occurs according to Maslow and others such as psychologist Carl Rogers in his "fully functioning person." Basically, job security and well developed social relationships are necessary or at the least facilitate psychological creativity and therefore innovation. Some studies show a direct link between job security and higher motivation levels in employees, and when employees leave a company the rehiring and training costs are expensive. At Lancaster Laboratories, a research and analysis lab in Lancaster, Pennsylvania doing $25 million in sales its 475 employees find life a little easier because of the daycare facility which is for both adults and children. This helps to meet some very basic needs of these employees and is a trend at many companies.

Keeping employees is done by respect for the individual as a human being. In the book *The Change Masters* Rosabeth Moss Kanter relates a study where she interviewed 65 Vice Presidents of Human Resource departments and asked them to identify the companies they thought had the best practices towards employees. She then examined the financial performance of those companies compared to similar competitors and found significantly better long term financial performance in the companies with the best employee practices. Costco is such a company. Even though they pay higher than average wages and provide 90% of full health care coverage, their revenues have grown by 70% in the last 5 years, and stock value has doubled (2010).

Some companies have a high percentage of employees that own stock in the company such as Genetech where 98% of the employees own company stock. When Science Application was a 20 year old company with $1 billion a year in sales of airline bomb detectors, CEO Robert Beyster said that all the equity capital the company needs it gets by selling stock to its 10,000 employees. People who feel they have job security not only invest money in the company but also effort. Companies like Hewlett-Packard and Polaroid have long had policies of continuous employment.

LISTEN TO EMPLOYEE OPINION

Whatever one man is capable of conceiving, other men will be able to achieve. ~ Jules Verne

One way CEO Jack Welch of GE kept ideas coming was something he called the "work out." Employees from different functions go away to a hotel conference center and are broken down into groups of 8 to 12 people. They then work on different problems for three days. After that a senior manager goes out in front of them and has up to a hundred questions put to them from the groups which must be answered either yes or no, or ask for more information. The manager has to answer right then and can not get help from any other manager as to what they should answer. Not only does this release a lot of information from the groups but forces managers also to reveal opinions.

Seek the opinions of your employees about names for new products and how to produce new products or improvements in any area. Create questionnaires for every specific area of your business and use them year after year. Economic genius Peter Drucker says every three years "put every idea on trial for its life." Regularly meet directly with the entire workforce to inform everyone about what is happening and tell them you need their help. Direct meetings with the entire work force at a location assures effective communication in two directions. Studies have shown that as little as 20% of what upper management is communicating is reaching the lower levels of the company. Also, if your standing right in front of an employee in a meeting they might be more likely to offer some input. Employees are a goldmine of ideas and vital to the innovative organization. 3M has obtained as much as 70% of sales from ideas obtained from their workforce. The State of Kansas pays employees for suggestions about their jobs, up to ten percent of the first year savings. The State of Texas has saved tens of million of dollars with an internet suggestion system. Procter & Gamble has an intranet site called "My Idea" which generates thousands of ideas. Their CEO told them "forget their 'Current Best Approaches' manuals and think for themselves. The core business is innovation." This echos Peter Drucker's comment that business has just two functions: marketing and innovation.

At USAA an insurance and banking business for veterans and their families they have a 95% participation rate by employees producing ideas, and in 2011 they produced over 8,000 ideas resulting in 247 patents for the company.

While companies must be open to ideas from outside sources, their most important resource is their own employees:

1. Your employees are the most informed about your business and will be responsible for literally transforming your company.
2. Your employees know the most about the "needs" of your company.
3. Employees have a psychological reason to help the company.
4. The company can easily access employees and they are a plentiful resource.

Brightidea.com offers software called WebStorm® that helps you get organized and is a system to make sure that ideas are recorded. It's a centralized location for your ideas where everyone can go online, make suggestions or take a look at what's happening. It's a very sophisticated suggestion system, where ideas can be given, reviewed by others, filtered, tracked and categorized. You can also create your own survey with free tools from www.hr-survey.com. You can also try Strategic Management Decisions that links survey items to business outcomes at www.smdhr.com. Eastman Kodak has the oldest suggestion system in the United States, and has been listening to employee's opinions since it started in 1898.

OUTSIDE RESOURCES

Two heads are better than one.
~ John Heywood, *Proverbs in the English Tongue* (1546)

In 2003 Henry Chesbrough wrote *Open Innovation : The New Imperative for Creating and Profiting from Technology.* This concept has companies using external sources for ideas in their innovation process such as: using customers to bring ideas into your company, licensing products or technology from outside the company, collaboration with academia, or using innovation consultants. Ideas can also go the other way such as open sourcing technology, and selling or licensing your technology to others. Adding the intelligence and creativity of many people and organizations together, results in a synchronistic whole that is greater than the sum of its parts, and beyond any individual part. Computers and the Internet are accelerating the phenomena of "Open Innovation."

Open innovation, also called open source innovation, user innovation, or collaborative innovation is in itself an innovation and the latest technique used by companies in the area of innovating. GE's ecoimagination® was an open challenge to innovators, business, and students to co-create ideas for energy in the home and the resulting ideas have generated $70 billion in just five years (2011). Anyone can use *Open Xerox* to experiment with technologies being developed by Xerox around the world such as *Mr. Taggy* that lets you find useful things on the web, or their *Aesthetic Image* search that uses algorithms to rate the quality of photographs. BMW teamed up with Local Motors, an open innovator for car design, and created the Urban Driving Experience Challenge. Winner Cosmin Mandita of Romania won a $7,500 cash prize and will travel to Munich, Germany to have lunch with the Managing Director of BMW Group Research and Technology. His concept is a system that activates street lights only while the vehicle is approaching and driving by, with lights out the rest of the time thereby saving energy.

Audi AG integrates with the public and academia in order to promote the influx of well qualified engineers into the automotive industry and funds collaborative projects such as their project with the University of Stuggart that does research on engines and light weight construction. The Audi Production Award is an international competition in which Audi AG gives scientists, students, and engineers worldwide the opportunity to develop visionary ideas.

The food products company General Mills worldwide innovation network (G-WIN) seeks partners to deliver innovation in the following categories: products, packaging, processes, ingredients, technology, and digital marketing technologies.

Dell Computers allows interested persons to submit ideas at www.ideastorm.com where they have had over 18,000 ideas submitted, implementing over 500 ideas into products and services at Dell. Top contributors receive no monetary reward but are given recognition by being listed on the IdeaStorm website.

"Bottom line" business people find it hard to believe that some people would give out product or service ideas freely, nevertheless, altruistic people do exist and may also enjoy the quality of commercialization that is brought to their idea. There is also financial investment made to commercialize the idea and the user benefits by having his needs financed by someone else. Users also gain psychological satisfaction by having their ideas brought to fruition. As long as both parties benefit in some way (your business and the user) the psychological transaction is completed.

You can co-invent with customers, suppliers, outside inventors, academia, social groups or clubs, technologists, statisticians, governments, radical economists, and futurists. As noted in a previous section, users are largely responsible for new ideas of major types or first of type. Users are not only individuals but they are also large companies. You can potentially become involved in shared projects with companies outside your business and possibly even competitors. In the new model of "Open Innovation" you must learn to avoid the fear of working with others outside your business. Be careful not to be too overly protective of your patents and ideas and consequently miss opportunity. Von Hippel of M.I.T. has shown that mutual trading of secrets can be beneficial and therefore, mutual benefit should always be the defining criteria.

Additionally, lead users are actively modifying and developing products. It was an attorney that developed a table saw called "SawStop" which turns off so fast it avoids an injury if your finger hits the blade. These lead users are unique and have unique needs, sometimes more urgently than others, and therefore develop new ideas to meet these needs; a perspective not available in your business (and also suggesting the attractiveness of offering customization). Users may not know precisely what they need, and this process of developing something brings out ideas and desires. In other less urgent circumstances users still may find these urgently created developments appealing, allowing you to make it a viable commercial product or service.

At www.uclue.com you can ask a question about anything and offer to pay a fee for the answer, and you set the fee amount. You decide what answer to accept and give a rating to the person's answer. At www.yet2.com ask to be put in touch with hundreds of companies around the world that might compliment your business. They will evaluate what you're doing and match you to a possible partner who is interested. This could be a connection to a Fortune 500 company that you may never have found.

Find patents you can license and use at www.ideaconnection.com where you can find a alphabetical list of subjects including 101 patents for agriculture, 89 automotive patents, and 147 energy patents.

Chapter 4 – Notes:

CHAPTER 5: NEW ROLES FOR PEOPLE

AUTONOMOUS GROUPS/CROSS-FUNCTIONAL TEAMS

Many ideas grow better when transplanted into another than in the one where they sprang up.
  ~ Oliver Wendell Holmes Jr. - U.S. Supreme Court Justice

All for one, and one for all.
  ~ Alexandre Dumas (1802-1870) *The Three Musketeers*

Bureaucracy is a sure killer of innovation. Groups free of rigid bureaucratic rules have the flexibility necessary for creative thinking. Members of the group should be made up of persons with involvement in a particular area, that is the users, and made responsible for something in line with the company's goals. The key feature of these teams is being as diversified as possible and at the same time being as small as possible. People from other areas of the company that are somehow related to the project should also be included. These employees from different functioning areas of the company are put together and focus on process. Instead of one function occurring at a time such as design, then engineering, then manufacturing, and so on, all these separate functions work together as a team following the entire process from beginning to end. The concept of specialization was one of the great insights of Adam Smith in his book *The Wealth of Nations* published in 1776. His concept is still valid in the new model where it is expanded to include specializations working together. Now, process, instead of function, becomes the organizational structure. This idea was advocated by Melvin Anshen a professor with the school of business at Columbia University in a *Harvard Business Review* article called *The Management of Ideas* the July/August 1969 issue. Professor Anshen stated that "change itself becomes the central object of management attention." However, he saw traditional business organizations as incompatible with the even then rapid level of change. His solution was a "project oriented" [read process] structure which he said "offers the important advantages of tailor made design to fit unique tasks, flexible resource commitments, defined termination points, and an absence of enduring commitment that encourages resistance to innovation."

More recently, Michael Hammer, a former MIT computer science professor has advocated this process orientation. In 1987 he coined the term "re-engineering" to describe the reorganization of companies around process instead of functions. This concept has a theoretical basis in George Land's transformation principle of "growth through different forms of linking behavior," one of his three principles of transformation in his book *Grow or Die*.

This cross-functional team concept helps integrate the functioning of the project, gives perspective where it is needed, brings expertise to details, creates stimulation in thinking, and provides a synergistic effect. The members of the team are like the artist who looks at an art piece, and gets feedback on the developing design, and builds on that feedback. The teams literally reinvent the company on a ongoing basis. The description the team is building in solving the problems of the company gives them all constant feedback which they use to make corrections in thinking, allowing them to move faster toward a solution. Consensus thinking is highly effective if handled properly (see section on group behavior). The cross-functional team is one of the most revolutionary concepts in business since the industrial revolution (also called simultaneous engineering in the automobile industry, and responsible for enormous, highly measurable productivity gains). Cross-functional teams should become the basic problem solving/performance unit of the business. Teams developing process innovations (also called core process redesign) saved $400 million of fixed costs in 3 years at Union Carbide. Des Curran was a 3M engineer that traveled the world with the title of "Ambassador for Innovation." Mr. Curran's job was to speak about innovation to 3M employees. In February 2000 he told the *London Times* "One of the things we learned about working on a new product is the importance of cross-functional teams." Mr. Curran is himself the creator of a fold-able respirator.

Management must get a new mind set in order to support the new model of the cross-functional team. Kanter's study of innovation in *The Change Masters* found the most significant relation between corporate culture and innovation was collaborative managers. In the classic post World War II model, business completed a part of the business process under one functional group and then "threw it over the wall" to the next functional area, until the customer was the last person to have it thrown to them. Managers worked mainly with the people under their supervision. In the new model, managers will need to work effectively with people from other areas who are not under their supervision. It is vital that they share power and authority with other managers in a spirit of cooperation and teamwork. The most effective groups learn to rely on each others strengths. In order to facilitate this new model it will also be necessary for employees to have direct access to a wide range of the company's information and data. Rather than going through some circuitous route, the information coming in that is related to the team's project should go directly to them. General Mills Inc. has organized 60 of their beverage plants into 20 person work teams acting as business units, and receive all necessary information. "They have at their fingertips all the data that would normally be held by management" according to Human Resource Director Daryl D. David. General Mills cited significant productivity gains and has instituted the concept at other plants.

To "make it happen"give full financial disclosure to your

employees. Specify rooms or areas that are available for these groups to use in order that it will encourage groups to meet spontaneously. Following the focused/unfocused method they will be working toward the company's goals. Some groups may develop specific expertise. These group can work as outside consultants giving help and expertise to other company groups such as opinions on projects or alternative plans or offer their own prototypes. Some company's groups forgo their profit sharing to gain bonuses on the specific project they worked on. These groups may be semi-permanent or limited in time and scope by gateways (defined "stepping stones" on the path to your goal) or termination points, or reorganized when needed. John Sculley, previous CEO of Apple Computers (now with Sculley Brothers) says most groups will probably last no more than five years (or until the project is completed). If it becomes necessary, a decision may be made to change the group make up in order to guarantee the stimulation of creative thinking. Care should be taken that groups don't become institutionalized, or used where they are inappropriate, such as when an individual has far more expertise than anyone in the group. Natural mechanisms will see that poor or ineffective ideas and projects will fail. Cooperation and "buy in" must be obtained from a wide group of people for resources, information, and support. Even though the corporate culture supports innovation, a bad idea should fail by not making it through the support structure.

Many companies such as Ford are using groups known as quality circles. These are members of a specific area who get together, sometimes with a supervisor, to discuss ways to improve the quality of products, services, or processes (at Ford they're called employee involvement groups or E.I.). These groups must be recognized as a part of the political system in the company and process related. Informational support should be provided. Although they do not have authority to change core ideas in a major way, they must be recognized as providing important ideas which should be implemented if possible. Many of the advantages found with autonomous groups are things related to increased motivation in the employees. Many studies (Martin Marietta Corporation - Michaud Division, Ford and others) show decreases in absenteeism, reduction in safety accidents, and reduction of grievances. Marvin Weisbord, a consultant on organizational development, has found that self management usually results in "40% increases in output per man hour."

At the Saturn plant in Spring Hill, Tennessee employees were structured in small, autonomous business units with responsibility for budget, inventory control, and hiring. At Xerox they're called "micro enterprise units." The greatly admired ABB a Swedish engineering company is divided into 5,000 profit centers with their own bottom line balance sheet. CEO to 1996, Percy Barnevik thought this was the best way to run this gigantic company which had $40 billion in 2011 sales.

Because they are organized around process, the black and white film group at Kodak works around what they call "The Flow" referring to the process. Feeding into "The Flow" are independent business units in the company called "streams." At Sun MicroSystems autonomous groups are called O.C.'s or operating committees. The people at Sun responsible for distributing incoming facsimiles decided on their own to write software which allowed the fax documents to be directly transferred to the company's work stations. This O.C. saved a tremendous amount of walking around the company with this direct information transmittal.

Levi Strauss, the apparel maker has found that a team manufacturing system has increased the quality of their products through greater flexibility, people with a wider range of skills, and more efficient production. When computer giant Hewlett-Packard needed a new disk drive they put together a cross-functional team made up of a engineer, a marketing manager, and the general manager of the Disk Memory Division. Together, using a lot of rule breaking methods, they developed the ultra small drive (called Kittyhawk) in only a year, saving 6 months off the normal process.

At Polaroid a new medical imaging system was brought to market twice as fast as anyone thought possible. Why? Interdisciplinary teamwork in the lab. CEO I. MacAllister told *Fortune* magazine

"Our researchers are not any smarter" but they used the value of "each others intelligence." Boeing co-produced the awesome 777 and 787 wide body jets by including subcontractors, suppliers, and the airlines in on the process.

To be effective, cross-functional teams must learn to rely on each others strengths, define goals, and have a clear understanding that team members share both leadership and accountability. Legendary football coach Vince Lombardi said " Individual commitment to a group effort ... that is what makes a team work, a company work, a society work, a civilization work."

RELATE STORIES

If history were taught in the form of stories, it would never be forgotten. ~ Rudyard Kipling

The Journal of Organizational Change Management in its Summer 1991 issue promoted story telling as a good way to transform corporate culture. Stories about the job getting done are educational and motivational. They can be positive or negative. They are appropriate at any time. Harvard psychologist Howard Gardner, famous for his *Theory of Multiple Intelligences,* said "Stories are the single most powerful weapon in a leader's arsenal."

Art Fry at 3M® needed markers for several different songs in his hymnal at church. He tried using slips of paper but they fell out sometimes. So he took an unsuccessful product at 3M (an adhesive that would not stick very well) and turned it into the ubiquitous Post-it-Notes®. Mr. Fry was told by 3M's production people that a machine to produce his material would take 6 months to build and it would be very expensive, and anyway no one would want it. So he built it himself at home and had it in the factory and running the next day! This incredible accomplishment can be nothing but an inspiration to others who hear about it. Both the technical success and the psychological achievement are outstanding.

At study done by Xerox at their Palo Alto Research Center showed that repairmen were able to learn more about fixing copiers by sharing stories as compared to learning out of the repair manual. Stories relate technical advice, technique, sources of everything, psychological where withal, mistakes, tricks of the trade, style, procedure, competitive advantage, alternate perspectives, and efficient execution. There is a lasting benefit of the stories in their continuous example through the retelling of the actions. Humans can remember more detail and instruction when something is told in a story because they remember the story holistically relating one thing to another.

Stories can be used for any area of your business such as how a new idea was created, how adversity was overcome, how someone learned to work better with another employee, how solutions were found to satisfy a customer, or how somebody did something different to solve a problem. Amazon founder Jeff Bezo realized that people familiar with the book business were not interested in his idea to sell books online, and he decided to look completely outside of that industry for investment, even though people in the book business seemed like the logical place to find investors. He talked to 40 people who turned him down, and everyone from the book industry was in that group. Mr. Bezo is now worth about 23 billion dollars! Collect stories, write them down, they are valuable aids to your future success.

STAY AT OPTIMUM GROUP SIZES

The well-run group is not a battlefield of egos.
   ~ Lao Tzu, founder of Taoism

John Blair, an industrial economist, comments on innovation in his book *Economic Concentration, Behavior, and Public Policy* (1972). He found "The contribution of large corporations to technical progress has fallen short of what would be expected in view of their resources" and they had a "lengthy interval between the making of an invention and its introduction as an innovation." The size of large companies with all their insular layers creates an impediment to spontaneous action in response to market or other considerations. Layers of bureaucracy filter out ideas without giving them fair judgment.

Smaller companies have the benefit of greater communication, feedback, and flexibility which naturally facilitates innovation. The inherent problems of bigness can be overcome when big companies act like small companies. Peter Drucker told *Forbes* magazine "Elephants have a hard time adapting. Cockroaches outlive everything." The optimum size which works for divisions, plants, task forces, or various types of groups can be determined by example. 3M had a median plant size of 115 people and only three of 3M's plants had over 1000 employees. Corning had 3000 teams in groups sizes up to 15 people. In Japan a sales location for cars is called a "channel" and each channel gets 7 to 8 sales persons. This is also the average size of their work teams at their factories. While the size of any group is partially determined by the resources and skills available, and the urgency of the task, the point being made here is to increase awareness about group size. Bigger is not always better. Optimum size affords flexibility and greater interrelatedness. The integrated workforce is one of Peter Drucker's ideas in the *Harvard Business Review* for a successful business in the future. The higher levels of interrelatedness gives a propensity for creativity and innovation. Obviously a larger group provides more talent but it becomes more difficult for everyone to participate. A more powerful and effective leader can allow for larger groups, and you must just use your judgment to decide. At W.L. Gore, a company which markets a Teflon plastic insulation and other creative materials technology, Bill Gore believed with a group size under 200 there was a ensuing interaction in the group which leads to greater innovation.

At Ford Motors the employee involvement teams (EI) average between 6 to 12 people who brainstorm in the workplace. An additional benefit of EI: Ford and the United Auto Workers surveyed 748 workers two years after EI started, and found that 82% of the workers said they were satisfied working at Ford, compared to 58% before EI. In a study by Kim Clark and Takahiro Fujimoto, *Product Development in the World Auto Industry* (Brookings Papers on Economic Activity, no. 3 1987) they found the average size of a project development team in an American or European company involved 900 engineers, compared to 485 in Japanese teams. The most effective Japanese teams used only 333 team members, compared to the least effective teams which used an average of 1,421 persons to complete a development project. The smaller teams apparently worked to maximum synergistic effect. The Ford 1993 Mustang team consisted of just 250 people. A direct result of this team effectiveness is the average number of engineering hours per car by Japanese producers was 1.7 million hours, and 3.1 million hours for American cars. Consequently, average development time for new models is 46.2 months for Japanese cars, and 60.4 for American. (European figures are similar to American). The

Ford Motor Company's new approach to manufacturing started with the Taurus, and has changed these figures, and Chrysler has adopted new better techniques also. Chrysler developed a high performance sports car called the Viper with only 85 people on the project using simultaneous engineering. It cost them $70 million to bring this car to market in only 36 months. In comparison, it cost Chrysler $600 million just to revise their minivan in 1991.

"X-inefficiency" is something William Shepherd describes in *The Economics of Industrial Organization* (1979) as "the excess of unnecessary cost as a percentage of actual cost." That is, along with large scale business can come equally large scale excesses: too much middle management, materials being wasted, and even something like a name change, such as changing from Esso to Exxon cost millions of dollars.

In *Megatrends 2000* written by John Naisbitt and Patricia Aburdene, they report the success of group size at a Tennessee Trucking Company, Averitt Express. By dividing their 1400 member workforce into productivity improvement teams of 3 to 10 people, they increased sales by 38% and earnings went up by 48%. Again, while the size of successful work groups knows no secret formula, the purpose of this section is to raise the level of awareness about group size. While there can be no exact formula, it seems that group size must be such that the entire group can act synergistically with the most effective teams learning how to rely on each others strengths. Make the group as small as possible while still creating the composition necessary to do the job, and instruct the team to learn to rely on each others strengths for maximum synergy.

A study in the *Journal of Personality and Social Psychology* found that groups of at least three could solve problems better than even a much more capable person. A two person team can reap some of the benefits of teams using a minimum investment of personnel. Choose members of this two person "duo" who can compliment each others skills. Jon R. Katzenbach and Douglas K. Smith studied 50 teams and told about it in their 1993 book *The Wisdom of Teams*. Their final judgment about the size of effective teams; from 2 to 25 people.

CHAMPIONS

A champion is someone who gets up when he can't.
 ~ Jack Dempsey, World Heavyweight Champ -1919 to 1926

Don Frey wrote an article in the *Harvard Business Review* for the September-October 1991 issue. Mr. Frey was CEO of Bell & Howell from 1971 to 1988 and worked at Ford from 1951 to 1968 where he learned that "innovations are lost without champions."

While there are no exact models for champions, it has become clear that champions are necessary to the success of business ideas. Champions are people who by themselves promote a product, service, technology, or idea. CEO's are the designated champions of the corporate vision. Champions are essential to the success of innovations, and are more important than a business plan or strategy. The champion uses plans and strategy but is more flexible in creating new plans when it becomes necessary, literally making constant revaluation and planning. Any new idea has it's "flight envelope" that is, an area where it is most effective, and the champion has the flexibility, and unyielding persistence to find that niche. Once a champion has picked up an idea it becomes "their baby" and they have psychological reasons to see the idea succeed. Texas Instruments did a study of 50 failed new products and in every single case they found that the product had *lacked a champion.* In some cases the champion has discovered a problem and then finds a solution to the problem. This was the case with Arthur Fry who used slips of paper to hold his place in the choir hymnal but found them slipping out sometimes leaving him with a problem. Mr. Fry found a adhesive a work (3M) which basically had been a failure, because it had a low level of adhesiveness. This was what Mr. Fry needed though so he could pull the slips off without damaging the hymnal. Eventually, Fry's persistence as a champion of the product saw the Post-it-Notes® product reach market only after he built the first prototype of the manufacturing equipment at home, and passed around samples to everyone until people realized the tremendous advantage of the note pads. Today the Post-it-Notes product is a ubiquitous item in the office and at home, the result of 3M's acceptance of champions.

Champions like Mr. Fry must be allowed to cross normal boundaries in order to maintain the necessary insight, persistence, wholistic accumulated knowledge, and enthusiasm across development, manufacturing, and marketing. This crossing of all boundaries in the business process is the key feature of the champion concept.

Champions work at times without the explicit approval of upper management and at times risk their careers. Lee Iacocca (later chairman of Chrysler) was the champion of the extremely successful Ford Mustang during the early 1960's. There were 400,000 Mustangs sold the first year and customers were storming the showrooms (over one billion dollars in sales). However, Don Frey relates that he was told by Henry Ford II (grandson of the founder) that he and Iacocca had their careers on the line "if it doesn't sell." Even though the Mustang was to become one of the most successful models in history, Mr. Frey said in the *Harvard Business Review* that the Mustang would not have existed except that "Iacocca won the day because he doggedly championed the project." (Mr. Frey himself was the champion for the use of the longer lasting and safer radial ply tires at Ford Motors).

At Apple Computers the name used for champions is "evangelists." Here the concept of champions has transformed from a vague concept of style to a specific job description. A formal policy should exist that allows people to voluntarily champion any important new idea.

Once in a while champions have come in pairs of brothers like the Lilienthal brothers (aviation pioneers), the Wright brothers (inventors of the first successful airplane), the Lougheed brothers (later called Lockheed, they were aircraft manufacturers), the Dodge brothers (early automobile manufacturers) and the Lumiere brothers (cinematography pioneers) whose first public showing of a cinematic film happened in 1895. (Edison originated the movie, what he called "kinetoscope" in 1888 and had a first public showing in New York in 1896).

ROLE FLEXIBILITY

The measure of intelligence is the ability to change.
　~ Albert Einstein

An M.I.T. study on the car quoted one CEO at Honda saying he wished everyone could work in one big room to facilitate the effective flow of ideas from one area to another. AT IBM they have the 5 year IBM Fellow. This is a position which allows an employee to work on any idea in any part of the company. Usually, everyone in the company is working toward the same goal and a person crossing boundaries is able to bring a holistic sense to what is happening. Also, occasionally people must enter into new situations for change to occur. When they should do this is just a matter of judgment but Sam Walton forced this change by allowing people to work for a period of time in a different position. Be a company that asks their employees to "make it happen" and then back this request up by having very loose job boundaries. Changing roles, jobs, positions of responsibility, and so on is a way to give a different and yet integrated perspective. According to the authors of the book *The Ultimate Entrepreneur* CEO Ken Olsen had 24 of the top Digital Equipment Corporation executives out in the plant one day assembling computers with screwdrivers.

At IBM Credit it used to take anywhere from 6 days to 2 weeks to get a request for credit processed, getting passed from department to department. Two managers decided to walk a request all the way through the process and discovered it actually required only 90 minutes. Now, they have one person called a "deal structurer" who performs the functions of each department to handle a single request. IBM Credit is now able to handle 100 times the amount of requests they used to handle.

If a person is allowed some freedom in crossing boundaries then they are able to bring a continuity to the problem or task they are working on. When that person has to turn that task over to someone else then we are losing some of the learning that has occurred. The new person may have to re-learn something that was learned already by the first person. Also a person following through with an idea has a greater sense of control and accomplishment, which is also a great motivator and sets the stage for greater "self actualization" (Maslow) which leads to greater creativity and innovation. Part of the success we have seen with champions is derived from the advantage they get crossing boundaries. It is a good idea to actually assign people to a wide variety of jobs over time. This gives them the inside knowledge of just how this area functions and interrelates to other areas. It also establishes the personal relationships necessary to the collaborative, integrated, holistic process of the innovative company.

BOOTLEGGING

First discussed by Kenneth Knight in the *Journal of Business* in 1967 with an article called *A Descriptive Model of the Intra-Firm Innovation Process*, bootlegging is an innovation process secretly operating in a company with no formal acknowledgment and no dedicated funds. To accommodate this important and successful process, sometimes called intrapreneurship, companies such as Google and 3M allow anywhere from 10% to 20% of an employee's work time to be devoted to personal projects. Google employees bootlegged *Gmail*. At Apple, Ron Avitzur bootlegged a graphing calculator program also known as *NuCalc*.

During the 1950's the very first video tape recorder was bootlegged at the American company Ampex by an unauthorized team headed by Charles Ginsberg. Instead of running the recording tape at ever higher speeds to obtain the high frequencies needed, they innovated a rapidly rotating recording head. The word bootlegging comes from the old practice of smuggling whiskey in the boots, and today has become to mean the unauthorized manufacture and sale of various products. In business it has come to refer to members of a company which go outside normal development channels to work on an unauthorized idea and possibly using unauthorized funds.

Radio Shack originally rejected the idea of a personal computer. Fortunately, a prototype was developed by a covert bootleg team. Don Frey said in his *Harvard Business Review* article that almost all the early styling and engineering work on the original Ford Mustang was performed with unauthorized "bootleg" funds. Robert X. Cringeley described in *Accidental Empires* how the innovative database language SQL was developed in secret at IBM and was finally revealed later to the top management.

At Toray Industries, a Japanese carbon fiber maker, they have an underground research policy called "angura" which allows a scientist to spend up to 20% of their time on discretionary pursuits which only their immediate supervisor knows about. Bootlegging is an accepted practice at companies like Xerox, 3M, Lockheed Aircraft, and others. When employees have a deep profound sense about what they can accomplish, but are unable to communicate the idea successfully to upper management, then bootlegging provides an outlet.

At Hewlett-Packard Chuck House bootlegged an idea even though founder David Packard was against it. House commented "It's said that I took great risks, but I never saw it that way. To me, the risk was in not doing it." (Gifford Pinochot III *Intrapreneuring*).

Art Fry at 3M bootlegged the first Post it Notes when he was told it would be too hard to manufacture. Today we have Post it Note® flags, memoboards, cubes, fax notes, easel pads, notes in business card size, correction and cover up tape, dispensers, and Post it Note® organizers. Mr. Fry's bootleg effort saved the company the loss of this valuable innovation. When to bootleg is a judgmental decision based on how strongly the members of the bootleg team feel about going outside normal corporate boundaries against upper management.

Totally discrete business units can allow for radical innovation in larger companies with pervasive bureaucracy. IBM's Boca Raton, Florida facility was used to develop their first personal computer.

Without any authorization, Jack Kilby at Texas Instruments created the integrated computer chip while everyone else in the lab was away on vacation. Also known as the microchip, and used in nearly all electronic products, he later won the 2000 Nobel Prize in physics for this invention. Bootlegging is confiscated power and is highly motivating as well as benefiting from a entrepreneurial style.

Chapter 5 - Notes

CHAPTER 6: TECHNIQUES FOR GETTING NEW IDEAS

RESERVED JUDGMENT: CONSIDER ALL NEW IDEAS POSITIVELY

Ignorance bids us stay judgment.
~ Andre Maurois, French author

Bond decided to put a decision aside, until he had more, and more expert, information.
~ Ian Fleming's character James Bond in *Thunderball*

In 1783 when Benjamin Franklin saw the new invention of the Montgolfier brothers, the manned hot air balloon, he was asked what use could be found for it. Franklin answered "of what use is a new born babe?" New ideas are just a beginning and are inherently incomplete, rough, raw, imperfect, sketchy, crude, unfinished, and only a beginning of the fully developed idea it can ultimately become. Therefore, this inherent quality of a new idea must be expected and accepted while considering the substance and essence of the idea.

In 1899 just before the beginning of the incredible advances of the twentieth century, almost nobody would have believed men would fly, go to the moon, or see people talking in a box (television) showing them on the other side of the planet. It is a natural tendency for humans to draw a conclusion with limited information, a survival feature that should only be used when we have a very limited amount of time available. Courts regularly reserve judgment until they have more information, and if time is available we should systematically use more consideration to examine new ideas. We are today constantly amazed by things we previously thought impossible. The author Arthur C. Clarke has said that any culture confronted by a technology beyond their understanding will consider it to be magic. Indeed, new technologies seem to appear as if by magic. The appearance of the LASER (an acronym for light amplification stimulated emission of radiation) is nearly as significant a development as the wheel. Dr. Theodore H. Maiman at Hughes Aircraft was given $1500 to make the first LASER, just because Dr. Maiman was so sure it would work. Bell Laboratory scientists had flatly stated that the Ruby LASER would not work. They should have stayed open minded because Dr. Maiman's Ruby LASER worked on May 16, 1960! (In 1960, Dr. Charles H. Townes, inventor of the MASER, a microwave version of the LASER, and Dr. Arthur L. Schawlow received a patent for a LASER with no working model. Dr. Maiman received a patent in 1967). This concept of the LASER was at first just a novelty item used as an art object, interesting to look at. Today there are thousands of uses for the LASER including the CD-ROM and LASER surgery.

Because any idea might be as important as the LASER or an invention such as the transistor, it is absolutely necessary to remain open minded and consider all ideas positively. The idea should be considered positively until proven. That is, it should always be assumed that anything is possible and any idea worth pursuing is worth continued consideration. Obviously, this is tempered by various factors such as time and money, but the idea itself should always remain as a possibility. There should never be a point at which an idea is considered to be proven impossible to accomplish. Many ideas which later became successful were at first not accepted. It was said of Robert Fulton's (1765-1815) idea for a steamship (in an age of sailing ships) that it was nonsense to attempt to sail against the wind by building a bonfire under the decks!

The American General Billy Mitchell (1879-1936) foresaw the military potential for aircraft and fought so intensely for it that he was court martialed for insubordination, and demoted to Colonel (posthumously returned to Major General). His instincts were right on the mark and the potential of aviation was clearly proven shortly after his death with the coming of World War II. During his lifetime most military authorities dismissed his ideas about air superiority.

IBM rejected Chester Carlson's idea for a copying machine. Today that machine is known as Xerox. The Xerox company itself didn't think making a color copier was a good idea until the Japanese companies entered the U.S. market with color copiers.

The world's very first electronic computer was ENIAC, an acronym for Electronic Numerical Integrator and Computer. The Radio Corporation of America (RCA) was offered the opportunity to be the prime subcontractor on a secret World War II military project to build the world's first computer. They declined because they didn't think it would work.

The research group at Xerox known as PARC (Palo Alto Research Center) developed the "windows" concept for computers, as well as the "mouse" control instrument. Xerox management did not see the tremendous advantage in these ideas, and it took Microsoft and Apple to bring these tools to the consumer.

Swiss watch companies rejected the revolutionary electronic quartz movement invented by Swiss researchers in 1967. During the following decade 50,000 Swiss watch makers lost their jobs. An incredible turnaround was performed by Nicolas G. Hayek the leader of Swiss Corporation for Microelectronics and Watchmaking (SMH) with 2007 sales of $5.9 billion (now known as Swatch). Known for the Swatch fashion watches, Mr. Hayek was quoted in an issue of the *Harvard Business Review*, "Too many of Europe's large institutions - companies, governments, unions, are as rigid as prisons. They are all steel and cement rules. We kill too many good ideas by rejecting them without thinking about them, by laughing at them."

Edwin Armstrong invented static free FM radio in the mid 1950's. This was at a time all the research work to date had said that static free broadcast was impossible! A French born American engineer, Eugene Houdry (1892-1962) created a process using catalytic agents to improve the amount of performance in gasoline. His process however, was rejected by the large oil companies for the reason that his engineering seemed unrefined and imperfect! These are examples of ideas as described at the beginning of this section, which demonstrate the inherent imperfection of a new idea. Instead of presuming a new idea to be rough and imperfect, the large oil companies rejected the catalytic agents idea specifically because of this quality. It must be realized that the more fundamental an idea, the more undeveloped will be its initial condition. All later developments and elaborations exist in the seed of an idea, and derive their origin from the initial idea, and all ideas must be approached with this understanding.

Some ideas are created with high levels of conceptualization and completeness, yet these ideas too will become more elaborate and developed. Some ideas are at first a failure but then are re-applied in a new way. At the company 3M an adhesive was developed which did not stick well but stuck a little bit. Basically, an adhesive that failed. Ultimately this low level of adhesiveness was applied successfully with the Post-it-Notes® products. Someone at 3M® was able to reserve judgment about a product until they eventually found a niche for it.

To further facilitate new ideas a formal process should be created to analyze new ideas. Additionally, there should also exist an informal process. At Matsushita (Panasonic) every six months a screening committee reviews recent suggestions. At the European electronics giant Phillips, the company has top division executives on a committee to screen new ideas in order to avoid interdepartmental rivalries. Tapping this national resource is an area that offers American business an opportunity to reap much greater benefit. At Toyota there is an average of 50 ideas per employee per year and Toyota has obtained as much as 20 million ideas in 50 years. Out of this a very high 95% were used by the company. At the largest consumer electronics company in the world, Matsushita (Panasonic), millions of ideas are created by employees. A partial explanation for the higher production of new ideas in the Japanese companies is the Japanese philosophy called "Kaizen." This philosophy is a personal program of continuous self improvement in one's life. This philosophy of Kaizen was successfully transferred to business in Japan. It is a system of incremental improvement. Little ideas that are just a little better than the previous concept. In other words, an idea that is fairly easy to create. It makes sense also that the person on the job might come up with a good idea for a small improvement, in an area where that employee is working every day. Experiencing a job every day can lead to ideas that upper management might never think of because of their perspective. Because this Kaizen process is continuous the products and services evolve more rapidly over time. Eventually the concept being developed becomes radically changed, improved, and transformed compared to the original idea. This high level of rapid incremental improvement is a key feature of the innovative company, and its implementation requires an openness to all employee ideas. Most of these ideas from employees may seem to be little ideas of little importance. In fact as we see from the Kaizen concept, many small seemingly unimportant ideas will eventually add up to a transformative change in the service, product, or operation of your company.

Employee ideas are a wealth of creativity and innovation and must be reviewed and analyzed or many good ideas will be tossed aside. This is the very reason why there must be a formal and systematic process. Very often these ideas will stimulate other thinking after analysis because specifically these ideas are related conceptually to those solutions which you do seek. There may be intuitive understanding in the ideas that at first are not readily obvious. So, you must give all these ideas the benefit of doubt for awhile.

When Thomas Edison invented the phonograph he demonstrated a sense of optimism and possibility during the process. While working on a telephone speaker for transmitting telegraph messages, instead of sending sound he heard the sound "halloo" played back. He had hollered through a diaphragm with a stylus-tipped speaker running over a paraffin strip. When he pulled the strip back through he heard a sound which was vague and almost totally indistinguishable. However, his notes at the time said "there's no doubt that I shall be able to store up and reproduce automatically at any time the human voice perfectly." His statement shows incredible optimism considering the indistinguishable sounds he heard. Here the great Thomas Edison (1093 patents; more than any other person in his lifetime and only recently exceeded) demonstrated an infinite ability to see the "diamond in the rough," the very crude, imperfect, and incomplete idea as it might eventually become. This sense of understanding is something that can be developed and comes with a close understanding about how innovation works. Nearly all of Edison's inventions started out with just the seed of an idea and were initially extremely crude.

Leonardo da Vinci (1452-1519) wrote that "once an idea is created you have also created all its parts." Surely one of the greatest minds in the history of man, Leonardo understood the simplicity and primitiveness of a new idea and at the same time saw the potentiality of it.

RECOMBINE EXISTING CONCEPTS

The most exciting phrase to hear in Science, the one that heralds new discoveries, is not "Eureka!" but "That's funny."
~ Isaac Asimov, prolific author

There are no facts, only interpretations.
~ Friedrich Neitzsche, philosopher

Electricity is really just organized lightning.
~ George Carlin, philosopher and comedian

The purpose of recombining existing concepts is to develop new perspectives as well as take advantage of serendipity. Place old ideas, projects, departments, tools, services, equipment, techniques, people, resources, goals, and any variety of concepts into a new conceptual framework and discover new ideas. This requires a tolerance for ambiguity in order to combine seemingly unrelated concepts in the mind, and see the advantages of the combination. Of course when you start looking for these combinations some of them seem just made for each other. General Electric uses medical scanning equipment to examine aircraft engines for gas cracks or defects of any kind. In this case we see two very distinct and different divisions within GE combining idea and purpose to achieve safety in aircraft engines.

As with most ideas, they look obvious once the concept has been created. Nevertheless, simple ideas like marketing sunglasses together with the sun visor hat in a package is good marketing. Use 3" by 5" cards and write down everything you own. Then rearrange the cards looking for interesting combinations. Also use the cards to write down problems, or any new idea or suggestion, and then mix the cards around to reveal new ideas. Merrill Lynch combined existing services in traditional banking (checking, savings) with brokerage services to create its cash management account service. Banks can get as much as 40% to 50% of revenues from services they created beyond the traditional deposits and loans. You can transform any idea by systematically going through features and combining them with other concepts.

Combine concepts such as usability or purpose in different products or services. Take a list of questions from one idea and apply it to another idea or product. New research shows that creating unique new ideas is best done by individuals, whereas combining existing ideas is best done using collaborative groups.

SEEK MANY IDEAS

Be fruitful! ~ Genesis

A pivotal work written over two decades ago by George T. Land is *Grow or Die: The Unifying Principle of Transformation*. The dust jacket quoted Frank George, Head of the Department of Cybernetics, Brunel University: "I think of this book as one of the most important books that has been written in my own lifetime." Dr. Sidney J. Parnes, President of the Creative Education Foundation called it "a unique contribution to the study of creativity. It presents the most comprehensive theoretical base I have seen in this field." The basis of the theory is life must change (grow) or in Darwinian terms be selected out (die). Land says "it is crucial to our examination of growth to regard information as literally a form of energy, the fuel for the engines that carry the processes of life forward to increasingly higher levels of organization." Here we see information described as the fuel of engines that produce ideas. The faster and further we want to go the more fuel we need.

Linus Pauling, was an American chemist who won the Nobel Prize for working on chemical bonds and also won the Nobel Peace Prize. When asked how one can get a creative idea, he answered that a person needed to generate a lot of ideas, to get just one single good idea. Dr. William Shockley was the co-inventor of the transistor, recognized as one of the most important inventions of the twentieth century, he shared a Nobel Prize for it in 1956. In his 1976 paper to the Institute of Electrical and Electronics Engineers he describes what he calls "creative-failure methodology." This was his method for getting creative hunches by having numerous bad hunches which led him to the creative idea. The business consultant firm Booz, Allan, & Hamilton found in a study called T*he Management of New Products* (1964) it took approximately 100 promising ideas to get one product. This product was the easiest to bring to commercialization on a time line evaluation process, however, this pressure to bring to market may miss some of the best products. The 100 to one ratio was observed by them across many markets. In a study done at the McCombs School of Business (2012) one group of subjects were told to produce quality creative ideas, while another group was simply told to produce high quantities of ideas. The group trying to produce high quantities of ideas wound up producing the highest quality creative ideas. Regardless of the reason for this, it points out the necessity of obtaining high amounts of ideas. It seems that getting the ideas to flow is the key factor, creating an abundance of ideas from which to choose.

Some ideas are obtained by serendipity. An ad for GE once said "you never know where your next idea will come from!" During the 1950's Dan Fox at GE was looking at liquid polymers when a cat knocked over some beakers and the concept of engineered plastics was accidentally discovered! Just looking for ideas can produce tremendous results. Simply producing ideas will automatically produce ideas of benefit to the corporation. This is what previous CEO of IBM John Akers meant when he said that R & D is like a well that you pour water into (money) and draw water back out when you need it. You put something in and you get something back of benefit. (IBM received a record 6,478 patents in 2012). This is the essence of serendipity; just as the Princes of Serendip sailed the world without anything in mind, nevertheless they always found things of great value. By the very act itself of searching, ideas of benefit seemed to be automatically discovered.

The giant consumer electronics company Phillips has invested heavily in research because they have a corporate philosophy this will guarantee them to automatically find new products. This has led Phillips to create vital technology products such as the compact disc or CD, the CD-ROM for computers, and the digital video disc or DVD.

The fashion watch company Fossil Inc. turns out up to 400 watch designs in a years time. They had $1.0 billion USD in revenue for 2005. In 1981 Honda motorcycles' domination of the industry was threatened by Yamaha. Honda's response was to create an astounding 113 new models in a 18 month period. Yamaha was over overwhelmed having turned out only 37 new models. Peter Drucker observed in an article in Fortune that the Japanese systematically develop three products to replace one product in order that at least one will be successful. Seek high quantities of ideas. Thomas Edison had 1,093 ideas patented which came out of surely an even greater amount of ideas. Today we remember only a few of these ideas, however, they are great ideas such as the phonograph (recorded music) movies (recorded video), and the light bulb. Just as the oak tree throws down many acorns and only a few start to grow and only a few of those grow into mighty oak trees, you must strategically seek a high quantity of ideas to get some mediocre ideas, a few good ideas, and maybe one really great earth shakin' idea.

This concept of many ideas should be explained to employees so that they understand that not all ideas have to be first of type; the "big idea." Any ideas might be beneficial to the company, even ideas that fail. There's an old story about a sculptor who created a magnificent marble statue of a horse. Someone asked him how he created this masterpiece, and he answered that he had "removed everything that was not a horse." Even when employees' ideas are not used, explain to them that they are "taking away from the horse" and this helps define the final goal of the company. Any attempt at ideas help define and also stimulate other thinking about what you're trying to accomplish, your masterpiece, and like a well you must draw ideas out of your people.

USE EXPERIMENTATION AND RESEARCH & DEVELOPMENT (R&D)

All life is an experiment. The more experiments you make the better.
　~ Ralph Waldo Emerson, American Poet and Essayist

There is but one sure road of access to the Truth, the road of experiment, record, and controlled reflection.
 ~ John Dewey, American Educator and Philosopher

The uncertain cost of experimentation should not be as frightening as the certain disaster of standing pat.
 ~ Don Fry, previous CEO of Bell & Howell

As previously mentioned, the return on money invested in innovation has been twice the return on money used for capital investment. Money spent on R & D must be considered a form of capital expenditure. It should be pointed out that pundits have continuously claimed that America was losing its technological leadership (that is, not innovating) while at the same time the process of invention in America continued unabated. In a study of patent activity called *Patent Statistics as Economic Indicators*, (*Journal of Economics*, Winter 1990) by Zvi Griliches of Harvard, Mr. Griliches analyzed patents and R&D investment by corporations. This was a very careful assessment of the situation including studying other papers and determining things such as drops in patents granted when there were fewer patent examiners. He concluded "The relationship between R & D and patents is close to proportional." In other words he is saying money invested in R & D provides results for the company. Mr. Griliches's further studies over many years have supported this finding. In fact, companies which create patents with more citations to scientific works, and more citations to other patents, and citing the most recent patents, are the companies on the leading edge of technology, and their markets.

A man named Chester Carlson had an idea in his mind. Like many visions of the mind it was somewhat vague and ambiguous. By performing an experiment on his kitchen stove at home he made real his idea for a copying machine. His first copy said, "10-22-38 Astoria" which was the date of the experiment and the location of his apartment, in Astoria, New York. Ultimately this experiment became known as the Xerox copier.

Edison experimented with over 2,000 different materials for the electric light bulb filament. Edison had a man who toured the world looking for new substances to try as a filament. Instead of just talking about an idea, Henry Ford was one to take action with an experiment. His experiment pulling a car along on a rope while men tried to do assembly work, was the precursor to the incredible advantage he reaped with the automobile moving assembly line. Eventually, Ford's net worth (adjusted for inflation) was an incredible 188 billion dollars!

At Xerox's Palo Alto research center (PARC) their concept of R & D is called pioneering research. This is a concept of basic research combined with applied research, and a focus on both process and product. They believe this gives them the best of both worlds. In the past there has been too much planning without taking any actions. The idea that taking action was better than endless planning was one of the features of successful companies identified in Peters' and Waterman's book *In Search of Excellence*. Hard cold reality is a quick teacher and defies and refutes contrary thinking made through planning. Art Fry at 3M was told his idea to manufacture Post-it-Notes® was much too expensive and too difficult. He took action and went home the next day and did it himself. Henry Ford was repeatedly asking his engineers to pour an engine block in one piece. They figured and figured on paper and repeatedly for months told him it was impossible to do this. One day Henry Ford got fed up with the situation and the multi-millionaire went down to the River Rouge foundry and poured the single piece block himself! Ford made possible in one day what his engineers had been telling him for months was impossible.

Experiment applies equally to process and trial runs with role playing can be used to try new ideas for services. Then the concept can be tried in limited areas. McDonald's tried table service in some of their locations. One of the other benefits of research and experimentation is the thing called serendipity. This is some fortunate discovery made while looking for something else or while just searching like in basic research. Dan Fox at GE accidentally discovered liquid polymers in 1953. In 1938 a DuPont scientist named Roy Plunkett was researching refrigerator gases when he noticed a empty cylinder had become lined with a white waxy substance. His curiosity led him to discover Teflon®, the slipperiest substance in the world. In 1956 a lab worker at 3M accidentally spilled a new chemical on her tennis shoes and later noticed the area where the chemical had covered was not getting dirty. Out of this serendipity came 3M's Scotchguard® protectant. Natural rubber from trees had always been looked at as a curiosity. You couldn't use it for anything because even though it had interesting properties, it would break when it got cold and turn very sticky when it got hot. When the American inventor Charles Goodyear accidentally dropped a sulfur-rubber mixture onto a hot stove, he discovered the effect later called vulcanization which allowed rubber to work effectively under different temperatures. Serendipity is a bonus paid to you simply because you made the effort to search for something. It is a process of discovery combined with preparation.

Through experimentation IBM invented the scanning tunneling microscope (STM) to examine magnetic discs. This instrument which can see the effects of individual atoms almost immediately applied to a whole host of applications in non-computing fields which IBM had not foreseen. At the time a black and white photograph was shown to the media displaying a fuzzy looking representation of the letters "IBM." The astonishing caption at the bottom of the picture stated that IBM had manipulated 37 xenon atoms to spell IBM! This invention won for IBM their first Nobel Prize (1986) and was the beginning of the incredible field of nanotechnology.

In an increasingly complex and interconnected world, innovation has become one of the main pillars of business. MiniMed was a Sylmar, California company (purchased by Medtronic in early 2000) that controlled 80% of the market for insulin pumps with $200 million in sales in 1999. Then president of MiniMed, Terrance Greg told *Fortune* magazine he liked to put money into R&D because "This may compress our earnings a little bit, but it builds a wall around us that a competitor can't break." This idea of building a wall of ideas or patents around a product or service is also known as clustering. Gillette has a wall of 22 patents built around their shaver the Sensor®. Companies can build walls around services too. Dell computers has over 2,088 patents (2010) and many are related to their successful and unique direct sales model.

An article in *Fast Times* was called *"Experimentation Is The New Planning."* Some form of experimentation should be associated with all new ideas. A simple experiment can tell you a thousand things and reveal further lines of inquiry, as well as create new ideas.

R & D consists of three types of research and experimentation:

1. Basic research that searches for fundamental knowledge.

2. Directional or applied research that searches for solutions to a specific problem.

3. Developmental research that finds ways to better use an idea.

Include research in every area of your business including things such as production, marketing, design, distribution, and applications research.

PROTOTYPES

In just a few weeks time, several Microsoft product groups... built prototypes and demos, and found that it works and interoperates quite nicely. ~ Ray Ozzie, Microsoft CTO

Once again, reality is in many ways a better teacher than just conceptualizing. A prototype can immediately reveal information not easily obtained by thinking alone. Even though Art Fry was told his notes were difficult to manufacture, his working prototype proved different. Henry Ford built a prototype of his first car himself at home in his work shed. He was so absorbed by what he was doing he didn't even realize the car was bigger that the door to the shed. One summer night when it was finished he tore bricks out of the wall and took his car for a test run, and the start of a billion dollar business. Ideas for dealing with sickle cell anemia disease were discovered by Dr. Makio Murayama at the

National Institute of Health. Dr. Murayama built a model of the hemoglobin molecule made of hundreds of little parts which he manipulated to discover solutions. Watson and Crick built models of DNA in a double helix that met the criteria of scientific information they had previously determined. The Wright brothers started with engine-less prototypes and unmanned gliders before building their final powered model, the first successful aircraft.

Thomas Edison almost immediately built prototypes of his ideas, very often before he even wrote anything down, seeing the idea most vividly in the "mind's eye." He quickly invented gummed paper on the spot because he was getting glue on his hands.

Prototypes develop and improve just like other ideas. The inventor of the typewriter was Christopher Sholes. He started out to make a machine for numbering tickets when a friend of his, Carlos Glidden suggested adding letters. They patented the machine in 1868. After building some 30 prototypes they sold the idea to Remington & Sons, a firearm manufacturer in Ilion, New York. By almost immediately building a prototype you can quickly learn about what works and what does not work.

The idea to build prototypes applies to every area of business. At Fannie Mae the lender they put together a cross-functional team and went to Cambridge Technology Partner a Cambridge, Massachusetts consultant. They designed a prototype software program in just five days and then developed it over the next 6 months. It tells Fannie Mae how much profit can be made by mortgages according to varying interest rates and allows them to be more competitive. It computes the latest interest information every 60 second. That means if they wait over a minute to make a buy decision they need to ask for updated information.

Solidscape Inc. is a Merrimack, New Hampshire company that can help with rapid prototyping. In combination with Computer Aided Design (CAD) they can quickly build prototypes of physical models, using LASER "sintering" which builds three dimensional objects in layers (www.solid-scape.com). This ability to 3-D build is a revolution in manufacturing, accelerating the speed of new idea creation and review, and is currently being introduced as an option to the individual consumer.

After prototypes have developed into a workable idea it is necessary to decide on the parameters of the idea, specific list of services, or for products decide on shape, color, size, or features, and then stick to this description and get this thing developed and on the market. Differentiate here between making something that works, and variances in taste. Listening to customers you will receive specific descriptions to innovate toward, or you can be leading the market with your innovation. Decide what you want, make something that works and get it to market. Be careful that you don't build endless prototypes; build the prototype and use it.

Then develop it some more and then allow the market to decide about the product or service using limited testing. President of the National Academy of Engineering Robert M. White expressed this idea when he said "If we can get a product into the marketplace before we test and refine it to death, we will succeed." This same idea was echoed by Apple's Steve Jobs who always told his people "real artists ship." It is very important that you get to market quickly because other businesses are possibly or even likely developing the same idea. Many advantages come to you by being first to market.

Obviously, immense projects that involve very high start up costs means that your idea must be thought out well. You must "have in hand" so to speak, all the parts necessary to exercise the idea. For example, one consumer electronics company started to bring something to market without a key component properly developed (I'll refrain from mentioning the company). Once you have something that works though you need to quickly bring it to market to reap the advantages of leadership. American actor and humorist Will Rogers said "Even if you are on the right track you'll get run over if you just sit there."

CHANGE BASIC ASSUMPTIONS

The man who never alters his opinion is like standing water, and breeds reptiles of the mind. ~ William Blake, English poet and artist (1757-1827) from *The Marriage of Heaven and Hell*

In all affairs it's a healthy thing now and then to hang a question mark on the things you have long taken for granted.
  ~ Bertrand Russell, British philosopher, mathematician (1872 - 1970)

Another feature of psychological creativity is a willingness to challenge assumptions. Sometimes a company must challenge its own assumptions. A key feature of the innovative company is a willingness to abandon the status quo. NCR failed to abandon the electro-mechanical calculator, for the electronic calculator. A company must be prepared to abandon anything and everything: processes, practise's, cultural features, its key products or services, or its whole way of doing business in the face of new emerging realities, what Walmart founder Sam Walton called "a willingness to change." People and companies will tend to follow an accepted model which infers certain rules, assumptions or theories about what they are doing. Following a given model can lead to a consensus about what is right or correct, which in reality is out of step with the real world. The model being used is incorrect because of changing factors in demographics, society, technology, or whatever. Because this happens and is happening at higher rates of change in today's world, we must periodically challenge the basic assumptions the company is using. Peter Drucker says put every idea in the company on trial for its life every three years.

In the first part of the 20th century the automobile companies made the assumption that the market was divided only by different categories based on price. Eventually they changed their assumptions when they realized the market had further diversified into groups according to lifestyle, and lifestyle marketing was born. Toyota's Scion model car line is aimed at a specific lifestyle group.

McDonald's had always assumed that customers were willing to wait in lines to get their food. Indeed the original concept from brothers Richard and Maurice McDonald was to allow people to quickly pick up their food, using a simplified menu, in order to give speedier service. Today McDonald's has come full circle from the original concept by testing table service at some of their locations. Originally, before "fast food" all restaurants assumed people wanted to sit down and wait for a waitperson to bring a menu. The McDonald Brothers challenged this assumption. We see here a never ending circle of changing assumptions.

Instead of developing a part in their own R & D facility the Swedish engineering company ABB told a supplier the general requirements for the piece and asked them to develop it. The supplier came back with a part that was 30% cheaper than the previous design. Asked why they had not built this new version before, the supplier answered that they had never been asked for it. This is similar to giving an employee some goal to accomplish without specifically stating how to do it, allowing them to add in their own creativity.

During the first half of the 20th century the shipping industry assumed that to be profitable they needed to make the ships faster and more fuel efficient. Even though they focused on this and made improvements they still did not have a viable economic model by mid-century. At this point they realized their costs were a result of spending long periods of time in port loading cargo. Ralph K. Davies owned American President Lines and wanted to modernize. In 1958 he sent investigators to 26 ports around the world to investigate the acceptance and viability of using containers for shipping. They adopted the model used by trains and trucks; the container ship was born.

INNOVATION CUING

A lot of what we see in Vista has similarities with Tiger.
  ~ Michael Gartenberg, technology journalist

Successful innovations anywhere can be used as cues to innovation and transferred to your business or organization. There is a certain basic design mechanism that has superficial ideas on top of it, and this feature can be transferred to your services or products. It is this essence of the design that can be used as a cue to release ideas for whatever you are trying to accomplish. Find a successful innovation and look at the "why" of its success. What is happening? Look for this basic mechanism and use it in your idea. Identify specific actions and write these down allowing them to prompt your ideas. For services you should identify "triggers" which cause certain behavioral actions or performance, execution, or operation desirable for your service or product. Look for hints, signals, clues, indicators, or pointers to beneficial psychological effect. Even features on products can be transferred to services, or from services to products. On products you can apply a variety of movements such as inverting, enlarging or expanding, twisting, elongating, locomotion, movability, and paced or erratic movement. Study the innovation you have targeted to find clues. What beneficial effect or result occurs because of any variety of movement or action on the target innovation? Apply that to you subject. Variety in shapes can include porous, coarse, smooth, slippery, hooking, or any form or pattern. Look for these features on successful innovations to see how they work, what it is they do in context, and how it might be transferred.

Charles Babbage (1791-1871) is known as the "grandfather" of the modern computer for his calculating machines called the "difference engine" and the "analytical engine" both precursors to the modern computer. These machines provided data by turning numbered wheels (numbered 0 to 9) and by manipulating studs placed into different locations that allowed the operator to enter a code or set of instructions. He also used punched cards with sequences of instructions for input. Babbage first conceived of his difference engine in 1821. In 1836 he used innovation cuing when he adapted the idea of punch cards for input control on his analytical engine. This concept (punch cards) was invented by Frenchman Jacques de Vaucanson in the 1700's and developed and improved by Joseph Jacquard to control cloth looms. This allowed automatic control of intricate cloth patterns. Later, Herman Hollerith used punched cards for tabulating on the 1890 U.S. Census. In 1924 he merged his tabulating machine company with others and formed International Business Machines, today generally known as IBM.

German engineers Gottlieb Daimler and Wilhelm Maybach together developed and sold the first practical automobile in 1892 (fellow German Karl Benz received a patent for an automobile design in 1886). Daimler and Maybach's four stroke internal-combustion engine was fueled by gasoline using a new carburetor design that injected a fine mist spray into the chamber, resulting in better combustion. Maybach had used innovation cuing when he saw his wife's spray perfume atomizer and transferred the idea to his carburetor. Today that company is known as Mercedes Benz.

Taplast is a Povolaro, Italy creator of plastic pumps, dosing devices and dis-pensive closures. They supply clients worldwide such as Lever, Loreal, and Revlon. Their history of innovation starts in 1968 when the founder invented and patented a tube cap that could also pierce the top (multiple use). In 1974 they innovated a tamper resistant cap (inviolability). In 1975 came the pump cap (delivery). In 1983 the child proof cap (user specific). In 1991 they innovated the dosing cap for liquids (precise measurement) and in 1997 the all plastic color cap design (design trends). These are six different core ideas that can be applied to your product or service.

In an utilization model of innovation ideas can be used repeatedly in different ways. The wheel is used over and over in many ways, as is the inclined plane. The LASER is also an idea we find being used over and over. Service ideas too are used in different ways such as the "frequent flyer miles" concept from American Airlines being used in a variety of services. You can apply any idea successfully in your company. Thomas Edison said " keep on the lookout for novel ideas that others have used successfully. Your idea has to be original only in its adaption to the problem you're working on."

Even making a list of innovations in your industry can stimulate your thinking and lead you to ideas similar to those innovations and yet different enough to be proprietary and maybe even a little bit better. This technique requires a tolerance for ambiguous relationships, so give every idea the benefit of a thorough examination. Systematic use of innovation cuing offers unlimited core ideas for product and service innovations.

THE INNOVATION PROCESS

For CEO's today it's all about achieving growth and efficiency through innovation. It's not about product innovation so much anymore as about innovating business models, process, culture and management. ~ Ginny Rometti, CEO of IBM

We live in an age of innovation. ~ Peter Drucker (1909 - 2005)

In the book *The Art of Thought* (1926) by Graham Wallas he suggests four steps in the creative process. In the same way I suggest four steps in the process of innovation. Obviously this is overly simplified, however it gives you a "handle" on where you are at in the process, and makes sure certain things happen and in the right order (while using cross functional teams). The four steps are:
1) Preparation
2) Experimentation
3) Prototyping
4) Commercialization

Preparation is identical to the first step in the creative process described in the next section. Even though you may already have already found a good idea, its background should be researched, analyzed, and discussion should be extensive. A broad perspective results in the best innovation. Be very knowledgeable about your subject, and also study concepts that are only ambiguously related to your subject area in order to create unique perspective. You should create notes and basic drawings. Legend has it the first Compaq personal computer was designed on a napkin in a pie shop in Houston, Texas.

The next step is experimentation to prove the viability of anything your not sure about. Try an experiment and just make sure you can actually do what you are thinking. Nothing elaborate here, just verify that all your ideas have a good basis in reality, and are not just wishful thinking. Do this for both products and services, using role play for services.

The third step is the prototype, again both for products and services. This is the complete idea in real form including all its subsidiary features. This must realistically meet the needs of the consumer, and all those ideas should be developed to satisfaction. This is a step where you must apply intuition and a sense of art. You can not just try every combination because just 10 things has a factorial of 3,628,800 so you must work on and develop your prototype using your intuition and judgment. The fourth step, commercialization, can not be the focus here. Focus instead on meeting the needs, desires, and anticipations of your customer. It is incredible that for the first approximately 15 years most automobiles had no side windows! The famous Ford Model-T is an example. In a rush to commercialization the auto builders did not truly consider the needs and desires of their customer. You actually had to go out in complete rain gear and drive your car while it rained in on you. If it started to rain while you were out somewhere you would be soaked because there were no side windows. This is the type of critical error that can be made and institutionalized if you don't have a process.

The last step is commercialization where you create the supporting network to produce and deliver the product to the customer. You design the manufacturing process or the processes necessary to establish your service. You line up your suppliers. Focus here on creating a finished product like everyone has seen and purchased many times. You are familiar with this although there is some variance between business offerings. It must look good, it must work right, it must have instructions, it must work repeatedly, it may have to accommodate different groups of people, it should have "the rough edges" removed in every sense. It should be comfortable, be packaged, and maybe even fun, come in different colors and even possibly have a name. Names such as Kleenex® and Weed Eater® have become almost generic terms, and their catchy names probably contributed to their success.

Create marketing material that will generate for you free advertising and word of mouth recognition based on the fact that you truly have something new. You must explain how it's new because you have been so close to it the newness has warn off from your perspective, however it will seem very new to the consumer. Register patents, trade marks and sales marks.

THE QUICK INNOVATION PLAN:

1. Write; talk; take action related to innovation.
2. Start using teams for everything and focus on process.
3. Get ideas from everyone in the organization; use an employee confidentiality agreement.
4. Start collaborating.
5. Listen to customers/ talk to employees.
6. Start the mentor/protege system.
7. Plan for change.
8. Write an innovation policy statement.
9. Budget a bare minimum of one percent of sales for research and development.
10. Predict something about your area of business. Something. Anything.

Chapter 6 – Notes:

CHAPTER 7: THE PSYCHOLOGY

PHENOMENA OF PSYCHOLOGICAL CREATIVITY

Man thinks. ~ Spinoza, (1632 – 1677), *Ethics II, Axiom 2*

To invent is to think aside.
 ~ Souriau, an early psychologist (1852 to 1926)

He was like a man who awoke too early in the darkness, while the others were all still asleep.
 ~ Sigmund Freud, writing about Leonardo Da Vinci

Imagination is more important than knowledge.
 ~ Albert Einstein, *Time* Magazine's Most Important Person of the 20th Century

The term "creativity" was first suggested in 1927 by Alfred North Whitehead in his paper *Process and Reality*. There are two types of psychological creativity that can be described: one is rational, linear in form and only partially spontaneous; the other is non-rational, non linear, and totally spontaneous, out of nowhere, bizarre, like a thunder bolt, sudden and mysterious.

Spontaneity is the key feature of the psychological creative act.

Remember what Author John Steinbeck wrote about innovation; the group never invents anything. The individual is where innovation first starts. At this point it is referred to as the phenomena of psychological creativity. All personality theories integrate creativity with different degrees of success. A four step linear process postulated by Graham Wallas in his 1926 book *The Art of Thought* is particularly helpful in understanding the creative act. These four steps are:

1. Preparation.
2. Incubation.
3. Illumination.
4. Verification.

1. **PREPARATION** (Wallas)

It is the purpose of preparation to prepare the mind with information. This should include historical, parallel, and information about the status quo.

There is generally a history to any subject, even if you have to go back as far as the myths surrounding it. Pioneering work is very important to study. Usually these channels of thought will have looked at the subject in a different way. Eventually out of pioneering thinking a comprehensive view of reality will start to emerge, and good ideas are lost to history at the point where they fall outside of this new emerging reality. Leonardo Da Vinci (1452 to 1519) invented the submarine, helicopter, parachute, aqualung, programmable robots, internal combustion engine using gun powder (placing it in a wheeled steerable vehicle), the airplane, and conceptual breakthroughs, protocols, and scientific techniques in many areas. All these fantastic ideas were unused for hundreds of years and his idea for the bicycle and the airplane were only discovered in 1965, misfiled in a library in Madrid, Spain (now known as Codex Madrid I and II). Therefore, studying the full history of an idea can sometimes reveal important invention, first of type ideas, avenues of forgotten information, and generally a new perspective. This new perspective will be necessary to see the familiar in a different and creative way.

In the early years of the automobile industry, electric cars, and ultra light cars called cycle cars, were two categories which at some point fell outside the realm of what was accepted as a car. Heavy, powerful gasoline engine cars became the emerging reality. Today we see micro cars (ultra-light) and the re-emergence of electric cars. Historical information may also contain an extensive financial investment in research. All this very valuable information should be studied in order to allow new matrices to form creatively and possibly find overlooked, good ideas. You gain the benefit of the tremendous amount of time and money invested in developing this information.

The Wright brothers (Wilbur and Orville) wrote to the

Smithsonian Institute on May 30, 1899 requesting information on the subject of flight. Assistant Secretary Richard Rathburn replied by sending four pamphlets on flying and suggested they read *Progress in Flying Machines* by Octave Chanute and *Experiments in Aerodynamics* by Samuel P. Langlely. The brothers also studied the work of Otto Lilienthal (sometimes known as the father of hang gliding). This preparation was the actual beginning of their great innovation the first successful airplane. In addition to this information being the fuel of their invention, the past mistakes made told them lines of thought to be avoided, and unexplored areas to be investigated. Certain basic concepts already discovered were also added to the Wright's basic knowledge. We must remember, from our perspective today the creation of the airplane seems straight forward and logical. However in 1899 it was a mystery and even seemed impossible to the Wright brothers. At one point Wilbur said it would be a hundred years before man could fly. Preparation was a very necessary part of the process of invention helping to create a framework of reality. The in depth analysis of Otto Lilienthal's work was eventually a rejection of most of his ideas while leading them to investigation and development of their own emerging reality.

Johann Gutenberg (1400 to 1468) used the parallel development of the machine used to press the image on coins to make the creative leap to the movable type printing press. He combined existing technologies of oil-based ink, improved paper, and the screw type wine press. His awareness of these existing ideas was essential in creating the moving type concept, a pivotal invention that changed the world.

Ultra successful car dealer Carl Sewell tells about how he got a good parallel idea in his book Customers for Life written with Paul Brown. Sewell was always annoyed by the constant paging for service representatives to pick up a car at his Sewell Village Cadillac. He had taken his kids to a Chuck E. Cheese pizza business that was very noisy with kids playing the games there. When your pizza was ready a chime sounded and you just looked up at one of the many monitors and checked to see if it was your number. He liked this idea and modified it and transferred it to his dealership. He has monitors also in the service bays so service technicians can receive information and also send data back to the service desk. His technicians perform 50% more work than the industry standard. Look for good ideas anywhere that might have a core idea that can be used in your business. Prepare for the creative idea by saturating the mind with historical or parallel ideas related to your subject.

Obviously it is necessary to keep abreast of what is happening and current in your field of endeavor to develop a leading edge understanding. The innovator is constantly preparing the mind for the creation of new ideas. Journals, books, magazines, websites, social forums, and conferences offer the most opportunity. Develop the information that is the fuel of your invention. In the movie *Deadline U.S.A.* (1952) Humphrey Bogart plays a big city newspaper editor. In one scene he tells another newsman in a rapid fire delivery "I want facts; facts, facts, and more facts!" The other newsman answers "the trouble is proving them." Bogart shoots back "Prove them later!"

One of the most far reaching inventions in all history is the radio. Inventor Guglielmo Marconi said "I read everything, absolutely everything I can find on telegraphy. I discount nothing. I discount no one, no matter how far fetched, no matter how simple-minded. I try it...at least once."

2. **INCUBATION** (Wallas)
The period of time following the preparation which allows the subconscious to form new and unique relationships is called incubation. It is a period of time when the person quits working on creating a solution to a problem and does not consciously think about it. Later, solutions and ideas seem to appear as if by magic. This mysterious phenomena definitely occurs even though we are not sure exactly how it works. Osborn (1953) found that later responses to problem solving tended to be more creative. While measuring incubation has been found to be very difficult, the anecdotal material supporting this concept is plentiful and the general opinion of psychologists (Kris, Kubie, Hadamard and

others) is that incubation does indeed occur. Jacques Hadamard writes in his book *The Psychology of Invention of the Mathematical Field* "There can be no doubt of the necessary intervention of some previous mental process unknown to the inventor, in other words, an unconscious one." In the book *The Act of Creation* by Arthur Koestler (1905 to 1983) he writes "during the 'period of incubation' the whole personality, down to the unverbalized and unconscious layers, becomes saturated with the problem." This is a problem that the person has remained open minded about, and has resisted what psychologists call "early closure." As long as the mind resists early closure there is apparently problem solving going on in the mind. Even the old saying to "sleep on it" suggests some unconscious process at work solving problems. One of the most famous cases of incubation relates how the mathematician Henri Poincare´ put aside mathematical questions and went to the seaside. He relates how he was walking on the bluff over looking the ocean when the answers came to him with "brevity, suddenness, and immediate certainty." Scientist Andre Ampere´ (the electrical term Amp is named for him) wrote in his diary "On April 27, I gave a shout of joy...seven years ago I proposed to myself a problem which I have not been able to solve...At last, I do not know how, I found it." Albert Einstein was shaving one morning absentmindedly looking into the mirror when "the most wonderful thought came to mind" about relativity. Regardless as to how incubation actually works in the mind's subconscious, it is recognized as facilitating creative thinking.

3. **ILLUMINATION** (Wallas)

This is the other side of incubation when the creative leap is made and the person makes the discovery with the suddenness of Poincare´ and Einstein. The most famous example of illumination is the story of Archimedes (287 to 212 B.C.) and the requirement by his king (King Heiro II) to measure the volume of gold in the king's crown. The problem was that Archimedes could not measure the intricate shape of the crown unless he melted it down to a definite shape, and of course he couldn't do that, so he had a difficult problem to solve. Later, while relaxing in a hot bath (an altered state of consciousness) Archimedes saw the water in his bath tub being displaced by his body going down into the tub. According to Vitruvius Pollio (famous for his Vitruvian man later re-drawn by Leonardo) in his book *De Architectura,* Archimedes' famous exclamation was "eureka!" a Greek word for "I've got it." He had discovered the concept of displacement and was able to measure the volume of his king's crown by the water it displaced.

In the cases of Poincare', Einstein, and Archimedes we can see that there was no logical linear pattern of thought, rather, the new ideas came to them during altered states of consciousness (ASC's) mysteriously and spontaneously. Einstein was looking absentmindedly into the shaving mirror. Poincare´ was experiencing the beauty and awesomeness of the ocean.

Archimedes was relaxed by the hot tub of water. Humans experience many different or altered states of consciousness such as fatigue, hunger, sleep deprivation, sexual experience, love, euphoria, psycho-active drug states, religious experience, transcendental experience, meditative states and many others. The time immediately before sleep and directly after are ASC's called respectively, hypnogogic and hypnopomic. Anecdotal evidence seems to suggest that ASC's facilitate creative thought. One afternoon in a library in England a man named Charles Babbage (1792 to 1871) was dozing on and off when he conceived of his "analytical engine," which was the basis in principle of the modern computer. The classical musical composer Wolfgang Amadeus Mozart was on an afternoon carriage ride, also in a hypnogogic state when he said he visualized "a complete symphony" including all the parts of every instrument. The inherent newness of illumination requires that the new idea is recorded immediately or sometimes it is forgotten. The English philosopher John Locke (1632 to 1704) said "The thoughts that come often unsought, and, as it were, drop into the mind, are the most valuable of any we have, and therefore should be secured because they seldom return again."

4. **VERIFICATION** (Wallas)

It is during the stage of verification that the creator demonstrates intellectual courage in proving the idea. Thomas Edison said that invention was "one percent inspiration and 99% perspiration."

Taking an idea to fruition is part of the creative process because the creator has the psychological state of mind that best understands the idea it created, seeing it in the "minds eye." Most often the creator of an idea is the person who can demonstrate the persistence necessary to go from the idea to a successful innovation. Alex Osborn was the founder of the Creative Education Foundation. He said "When it comes to creative efficacy, neither the extent of our knowledge nor the potency of talent is as vital as our driving power." Most ideas will be in a very elemental form and will require some development and maybe even extensive development. Edison's psychological persistence tried 2,000 different materials to find a filament to use in his incredible invention the electric light bulb.

Another person who offers us a basic understanding of psychological creativity is George T. Land. In his unique book *Grow or Die* he offers a powerful theoretical explanation of creativity that relates it to the growth process in biological systems:

1. Taking in information/biological nourishment (chemical information/preparation for Wallas).
2. Breaking it down to analyze/biological digestion (incubation for Wallas).
3. Putting it in new configurations as ideas/ biological assimilation (illumination for Wallas).

4. Evaluation for best idea/biological testing against genetic templates (verification for Wallas).

5. Taking action (also verification of Wallas).

6. Response to reaction with the environment.

If these functions do not all occur then Mr. Land says growth can not happen effectively. Indeed, all growth, even that at sub atomic levels works this way. Land states "The psychological process of living is to assimilate external materials and to reformulate them into extensions of the self." The availability of information and environment are the two things which affect growth.

Transformation is any distinct evolution seen through growth. Land has three transformation principles:

1. Growth motivated/evolving organized behavior.

2. Growth through different forms of linking behavior.

3. All growth is a function of information.

FEATURES OF THE CREATIVE PERSONALITY

'There is no use trying,' said Alice. 'One can't believe impossible things.' 'I daresay you haven't had much practice,' said the Queen. 'When I was your age, I always did it for half an hour a day. Why, sometimes I've believed as many as six impossible things before breakfast.' ~ Lewis Carroll, *Alice in Wonderland*

It is generally recognized by psychologists that intelligence described by I.Q. measurement is not related to creative ability. In other words, a person might be very creative without having a high I.Q. measurement. The following are the personality features demonstrated by high creativity:

1. **Spontaneity:** This feature is considered by the author to be the key feature of psychological creativity. When Pablo Picasso was asked how his paintings developed he said " in art there is no past or future, but only the present." Psychologist Dean Simonton says " In a loose sense, genius and chance become synonymous."

2. **Flexibility:** the ability to see things in different or alternative context, and the ability to adapt to changing situational demands.

3. **Risk taking:** crawling out on a limb to get the best fruit. An ability to balance the risk with the reward. The Roman statesman Cicero said " The greater the difficulty, the greater the reward."

4. **Lateral or associative thinking:** seeing relationships (DeBono introduced the term "lateral thinking" in 1967.) The human brain functions using patterns. Lateral thinking is unconnected to the linear pattern but associated in some oblique way to the subject.

5. **Tolerance for ambiguous relationships:** an ability to see the contextual relationship in seemingly unrelated concepts.

6. **Synthesizing opposites:** Carl Jung's seeing opposites simultaneously in the same context; Arthur Koestler's bisociation and the two headed god Janus; Bob Dylan has a line in a song about a preacher who wants your money and a banker who wants your soul; T.S. Eliot writes in *The Hollow Men* "Shape without form, shade without color, paralyzed force, gesture without motion."

7. **Visualization:** the ability to experience concepts in images such as Einstein seeing himself on a beam of light. He also used this to develop an important theory called *The Principle of Equivalence of Gravitation and Inertia.* In this experiment he imagined an unconnected elevator falling freely from a great height over the planet Earth. Inside the elevator, he imagined scientists performing various experiments. In one, the scientists take common objects from their pockets and release them. Rather than dropping to the floor the objects float as if there's no gravity. The scientists try to jump up and down but when they jump up they just float inside the elevator. Even though they are in the gravitational field of Earth, paradoxically, it seems as if gravity has been suspended. Next, Einstein imagines the same elevator deep in space and far removed from the gravitational field of Earth. This time the elevator has a cable attached to the top of it pulling at a constant rate of acceleration. Again a paradox appears. When the scientists drop objects from their pockets the objects fall as if in a gravitational field, and when the scientists

jump up they fall back to the floor of the elevator. It seems exactly as if they are in the gravitational field of Earth.

8. **Playfulness:** this relates to spontaneity and is also an altered state of consciousness. Anecdotal evidence indicates this to be a key feature of innovative organizations.

9. **Sense of the Future:** an unlimited openness to possibilities and the ability to merge possible future events.

10. **Intellectual courage:** consisting of critical rationality, resistance to enculturation, and challenging assumptions. When physicist Murray Gell-Mann suggested quarks as the building blocks of neutrons and protons other scientists thought it absurd, yet today it is a proven fact.

11. **Divergent thinking:** an expansion of thinking on a given set of ideas that resists convergent thinking while developing various aspects of the core idea.

12. **Reserved judgment:** a key feature of brainstorming and innovation. It allows for higher rates of ideation.

13. **Fluency**: high amount of responses and resistance to early closure. Ernest Hemingway tried 44 different endings in *A Farewell to Arms*. In a study done by psychologist Dean

Simonton of 2,2026 scientists he found that those who had high amounts of successful and respected works also had higher amounts of failures. These people simply produced more than others. Pablo Picasso was an extremely prolific artist producing over 13,000 works of art. According to the *Guinness Book of World records,* Paul McCartney is responsible for writing over 700 songs, and is the most prolific songwriter ever (Wolfgang Amadeus Mozart composed 600 classical pieces from age 5 to 35 years old when he died).

14. **Originality:** categorized as first of type, major improvement, minor, and incremental.

15. **Elaboration:** creating highly developed, embellished, refined or detailed concepts adding value to your idea.

16. **Perseverance:** Edison trying over 2,000 materials for a filament in the electric light bulb. On the Wright brothers monument at Kitty Hawk, North Carolina (site of the first successful aircraft flight) there is engraved the words "Dauntless resolution, unconquerable faith." Albert Einstein said "I think and think for months, for years; 99 times the conclusion is false. The 100th time I am right."

17. **Curiosity:** keeping a almost childlike sense of wonder and awe about everything. Einstein said "I have no special talent. I'm

only passionately curious."

18. **Transcendence:** Going beyond the usual rewards for doing something, and obtaining a supreme level. Surpassing all limits.

CREATIVE TECHNIQUES

1. **Serendipity:** simply searching produces results.

2. **Add ideas together forcibly:** a film was run over a Nike TV ad where a person was running. The visual is striking with part of the film showing on the runner's body.

3. **Take away something:** the lifting body concept for a aircraft mostly removes the idea of a wing. Systematically remove one concept after another, while using reserved judgment.

4. **See negatives as opportunities:** when 3M® scotch tape was first being used it was always sticking on the roll and was difficult to get off. An innovative manager created the serrated edge dispenser.

5. **Brainstorming:** features wild unrestrained guesses at the solution to a problem while using reserved judgment. Get a group together and give them a subject or goal. Write down every single idea. Some seemingly crazy ideas might look better the next day.

You might modify an idea later, but first get the idea (your raw material) and use reserved judgment to get them.

6. **Word association:** use a dictionary or thesaurus and rearrange words or concepts in different groups, using ideas significant to the idea you are working on. Use 3" by 5" cards with concepts in your business, and mix an match them allowing for spontaneous conceptualizing.

7. **Meditation and reflection:** these are altered states of consciousness that facilitate creative thinking (such as Leonardo Da Vinci staring at the *Last Supper* for two hours).

8. **Situational novelty:** place the product/service into different areas or situations. Try areas far removed from your area of business. Place any restriction or allow a specific freedom in the situation. Imagine a scenario. Put yourself in the customer's shoes for a new perspective.

9. **Manipulation of facts:** reconfiguration, assimilation. List facts about your business and then place them in new groups or orders.

10. **Metaphor and analogy:** compare to other concepts to find similarities between otherwise dissimilar ideas. The burrs from a plant sticking on someone's socks gave them the idea for Velcro® fasteners.

11. **Exploit incongruities:** Ray Kroc had a extremely large order for ten milk shake mixers that was inconsistent with what a small food stand would normally order. He investigated and found the McDonald brothers speedy food service, eventually turning it into a international business giant.

12. **Fantasy/daydreaming:** play "what if" or "lets pretend" such as when Einstein imagined himself on a light beam.

13. **Synthesize opposites:** merge opposites in a complementary way.

14. **Go beyond boundaries:** increase or expand, decrease or contract. Go beyond limits to find new limits.

15. **List the pro's and con's:** See both sides of the idea.

16. **Alternate perspective:** make video's of processes or services or products in use, and analyze. Put yourself in the users place.

17. **Morphological analysis:** Examine the relationship of the parts without regard to their individual functions.

18. **Reverse position:** use opposite viewpoint.

19. **Generate ideas:** then cluster in ways that make sense, then

place constraints on the idea.

20. **Sacred cows:** this technique questions everything.

21. **Relate to a specific human behavior:** some characteristic such as left handed people, blind people, short people, tired people, people in a hurry, people who like short cuts, someone always carrying something, and so on.

22. **Transform an Idea:** in a group, write down on idea and then pass it to the next person who must elaborate and pass it on. Eventually the idea becomes dramatically transformed.

GROUP DYNAMICS

Never doubt that a small group of thoughtful citizens can change the world. Indeed, it is the only thing that ever has. ~ Margaret Mead

The cultural anthropologist Margaret Mead recognized that small groups can create revolutions in thinking. The term "group dynamics" was first used by social psychologist Kurt Lewin in 1945 to describe psychological forces within a group. A non systematic approach tends to focus on the areas of previous success, and within the area of greatest experience. This leads to early closure and concomitant low levels of ideas. Avoid this by telling the group to be initially challenging. Assign one person in the group to deliberately take the opposite viewpoint of the group, the so-called Devil's Advocate.

The classic group case is President Kennedy's failure to get an accurate assessment of what became known as the Bay of Pigs fiasco. With the encouragement of the U.S. Military, Cuban revolutionaries in Florida planned an invasion of Cuba. The U. S. Military leaders and advisers mislead Kennedy by giving him the impression the invasion would succeed, and so Kennedy allowed it to go forward. They believed they could manipulate the young president into sending U.S. troops into Cuba once the need for additional forces became apparent. However, when the invasion failed, Kennedy refused to send in American troops. Some have unfairly declared him weak and indecisive, but Kennedy was wisely looking at the bigger picture. If the U.S. invaded Cuba it would give the Soviet Union the justification to invade West Berlin, and Kennedy wanted to avoid this potentially critical situation, one that could possibly lead to world war. The failure of the invasion led to the Soviet Union obtaining an agreement with Castro to place nuclear weapons in Cuba, leading to the very dangerous Cuban Missile Crisis. Kennedy later revised his group practices in order to encourage challenging thoughts, debate, and dissent. He once said "When at some future date the high court of history sits in judgment on each of us, it will ask: Were we truly men of courage … with the courage to stand up to one's enemies … and the courage to stand up, when necessary, to one's associates."

Normal group pressures leads sometimes to agreement on some point irregardless of the accuracy. A study done by Solomon E. Asch was frightening in its results. Asch, a psychologist, showed two lines of close but different lengths. Then he asked a group of six to agree to say the lines were the same length when they were asked again, and to strongly support that statement. Another person was then brought into the group as a naive subject. Each of the first six were asked if the lines were of the same length and they all stated they were sure the lines were of the same length. After hearing the statements of the first six people, the naive subject agreed the obviously different lines were of the same length! This group pressure effect was obtained an astounding 58% of the time. One of the ways to overcome these effects is to use a devil's advocate who always questions everything.

An interesting story related to this is the Dutch admirals. Two young men starting out in the Dutch Navy made an agreement; around other officers they would always sing elaborate praises of each other, and point out the good things about each other. Eventually they became the youngest admirals ever in the Dutch Navy. This was a case where people could be convinced of something because they heard other people repeatedly suggest something. Be careful that an idea is popular for the right reasons.

One very dangerous group activity which occurs is known as the "risky shift phenomena" also known as group polarization, or group-think. What happens is that each person psychologically moves their position to a more radical position than the previous person. This sometimes happens with overly strong leaders. This is some kind of attempt to over agree with them or out do them. As this process continues from person to person, it develops into a dangerous and irrational position and may rely on excessive rationalizations and inaccurate stereotypes. Understandably, the group is a team trying to work together to accomplish their goal and the tendency is towards consensus even if it is inaccurate. Instruct group members to challenge assumptions, and take breaks and return to the discussion at a later time. Keep the facts in front of you, and instruct members it is acceptable to disagree. President Kennedy started inviting outside experts to some meetings.

Basically, groups should move toward divergent solutions until sufficient ideas are generated and then use convergent thinking. Group make up should include as much variety in expertise as possible to give different perspectives. To start, according to the theory of growth developed by George Land in *Grow or Die,* you should initially seek commonality among members and then develop and share differences. Be sure to get everyone's opinion because silence by members of the group is usually mistaken for agreement. Be careful to avoid rationalizing, stereotyping problems, and overly optimistic conclusions. Nothing should be censored and all viewpoints should be allowed. Systematically consider all the alternatives, including previously rejected ideas.

IMAGINATIONAL THOUGHT

Imagination rules the world. ~ Napoleon Bonaparte

I paint objects as I think them, not as I see them.
   ~ Pablo Picasso

In order to better understand gravity Einstein used a thought experiment based on the idea of a freely falling elevator. He used this to develop the *Principles of Equivalence of Gravitation and Inertia.* In 1945 he responded to an inquiry from Jacques Hadamard about how mathematicians think. Einstein states "The physical entities which seem to serve as elements in thought are certain signs and more or less clear images which can be voluntarily reproduced and combined." He quite pointedly states that "language does not seem to play any role in my mechanism of thought." Visualization offers obvious benefits for efficient thinking such as enveloping many concepts into one single image or the complete freedom to break any previous rules or limitations. It is also effective in the holistic sense of accurately relating one part to another. Discussing visualization reminds one of the comment by Confucius, "a picture is worth ten thousand words." That's a ratio that encompasses 10,000 words to just one single image. In one sense, thinking in imagery is like a high speed use of words that is uninhibited by the structure of language itself.

The creative process can be simply stated as a destructive/constructive act. It moves from breaking rules and old concepts to constructing new imagery. This new imagery also constructs all the underlying concepts. Archimedes "sees" himself displacing the water in his bath tub as the constructed concept of displacement (the image is turned into language during verification). Another way to approach illumination is using thought experiments just like Albert Einstein. Surely many people already use visualization in many ways. We must be aware though that this is a important and highly efficient form of thinking. It is freer in the way it uses and relates information and therefore beneficial to creating new ideas. We should use this type of thinking more often for problem solving of every kind.

Thought imagery often proceeds illumination. If we consciously decide to use it we made aid illumination. It can be used to build prototype products or services. It can perform experimental surgery. It can picture a company in any of various operational scenarios. It can re-conceptualize every process in your business. You can test every idea in the "minds eye." A contemporary and sometime foe of Thomas Edison was Nikola Tesla. Tesla discovered the advantages of alternating current (A.C.), and promoted it against Edison's preferred direct current (D.C.). Today we mainly use alternating current, the main advantage being that it can be transmitted long distances without significant loss of power. Tesla was an inventive genius who could design a machine in his mind, start it to running, and then leave it. He said that later he would return to it in his mind to "see" what had happened.

Individuals must put to practice and exercise the use of their imagination in specific ways that relate to creative problem solving and the development of new ideas. It should be used after sufficient preparation. Preparation will start with reading, writing, and discussion. As you finish preparation you should start to use imagery to analyze changeable ideas. Later, after illumination, you turn the concept into language.

Imaginational thought is thinking with imagery and a plan. This is powerful wholistic thinking uninhibited by the structure of language. For this to be effective you must have a real Plan that has defined goals and objectives which define the path you follow.

ANTICIPATE/PREDICT THE FUTURE

I hold that man is in the right who is most closely in league with the future. ~ Henrik Ibsen (1828-1906) Norwegian poet

The best way to predict your future is to create it.
~ Abraham Lincoln

I conclude that the only thing for us to do is to continue to enlarge our vision as much as we can. Then we shall see.
~ Louis J. Halle, *Out of Chaos*

Microsoft's Bill Gates said "If your too focused on your current business, it's hard to change and concentrate on innovating." Some of your time should be spent predicting the future. It's been done many times and with great accuracy, and yes your business can do it too. Jules Verne predicted the electric powered submarine in *Twenty Thousand Leagues Under the Sea*, and that story also predicted weapons that shocked people (similar to the Taser). He also described going to the moon in *From the Earth to the Moon* published in 1865, over a century before man landed on the moon. In a 1901 *Scientific American* magazine interview Thomas Edison predicted molds used with poured concrete to build houses and today they are a reality. A 1918 issue of the magazine predicted driver-less cars, something being introduced today by Google and already approved by two state legislatures.

It is easy to predict that in the future humans will not be allowed to drive cars anymore because the GPS computer/radar controlled car will be so much safer than humans. You'll just get in your car and state your destination!

Every year IBM makes five predictions about the future that will occur in the next five years, called "IBM 5 in 5." 2012 predictions are:
1. Touch; you will be able to "touch" or feel things through your phone or computer.
2. Smart pixels; computers will be able to look at photo's and determine meaning.
3. Intelligent hearing; computers will analyze the sounds they hear, for example the sounds in ocean waves, the sounds in wood and other structures.
4. Computers that can taste; creating unique foods, or appealing foods for diabetics.
5. Computers that can smell; analyzing molecules from your breath to tell if you're getting sick or if surfaces are sanitary.

Technovelgy.com is a website that has the predictions of science fiction writers that are coming true. The great science fiction author Arthur C. Clarke predicted communication satellites in 1945. You can go to this website and find an idea related to your field and then use directional research and development.

You can always count on a long list of desires to innovate towards:

1) Things can be safer (airbags in cars).
2) Easier to use (pull tab can tops).
3) Smaller (entire field of electronic miniaturization).
4) Stronger (CNC or cellulose nano crystal is twice as strong as carbon fiber).
5) More convenient (ATM's).
6) Ubiquitous (wireless internet everywhere).
7) Niche oriented (products for left handed people).
8) Fun (Yehaa!).
9) Exciting (experiencing outer space with Virgin Galactic).
10) Emotionally immersive (3-D movies).
11) Physically enhancing (any hand tool).
12) Giving comfort (articulated bed).
13) Emotionally rewarding, (automatic donations when you buy something).
14) Faster (express check-in).
15) Versatile (the Amphicar could be used in both the water and on land).
… and the list goes on because the unique desires of humans is never ending.

Predicting what your customer wants is another aspect of innovation that compliments other means of developing ideas. When Sun Microsystems anticipated the markets' desire for standards and compatibility, they were able to take over the workstation market from Apollo computers by 1986. By 1987 Sun's annual fiscal revenues had jumped to $537.5 million. Henry Ford said if he just gave his customers what they wanted, all they would have asked for was "faster horses!"

In 1953, 50 years after the invention of the airplane, *Aero Engineering Review* contained articles looking at the progress of flight and looking towards the next fifty. While there was some feeling that supersonic flight might be possible, no anticipation was made about space travel. In just four years the world was startled by the launch of Sputnik I and the space age of exploration. Physicist Stephen Hawking said "Our greatest hopes could become reality in the future. With the technology at our disposal, the possibilities are unbounded." The failure to anticipate the future is quite simply a failure to believe anything is possible. If you believe time travel and anti-gravity machines are possible, then you have at least some chance of obtaining these goals. Otherwise, it is inherent that you will never reach for the idea. At one point Wilbur Wright doubted that man would ever fly even in one hundred years. In 1900 astronomer Simon Newcomb said "The demonstration that no possible combination of known substances, known forms of machinery and known forms of force, can be united in a practical machine by which men shall fly long distances through the air, seems to the writer as complete as it is possible for the demonstration to be." Then in

1902 he added "Flight by machines heavier than air is unpractical and insignificant, if not utterly impossible." The very next year the Wright brothers made it possible. What the Wrights did in overcoming their own doubts is what we must all do. Some of the Wrights' doubts were about engine power. Their first engine had 12 horsepower (some jet turbine engines today have as much as 40,000 hp). They never imagined or believed possible the massive amounts of horsepower generated by today's engines. If the limits of an idea or problem are holding you back then you must believe anything is possible, and approach your problems with that attitude. In order for a flying machine to be invented, the Wright brothers had to develop a powerful enough engine even though they first doubted it possible.

Seldom or never is there any limits to growth and development. When it became impossible to film objects smaller than the wave length of light, they made it possible by using shorter wave length X-rays to film objects. This basic concept of no limits to growth and development means we should always believe things will become more efficient, bigger, faster, slower, easier, smaller, more intelligent, and possible.

Publisher Henry R. Luce founded *Time* magazine, *Fortune*, and others and was one of the most influential persons of his day. He said "Business, more than any other occupation, is a continual dealing with the future, it is a continual calculation, a instinctive exercise in foresight." He points out that business is all about the Future and it is the business person's job to regularly and continuously address this fact using our judgment and intuition. We help define this by following our desires and enabling them.

In the 1600's when it took weeks to cross the ocean between Europe and America, it would have seemed impossible to make the trip in just a few hours, and yet in jet airplanes we have been doing this now for decades. Even now it seems almost impossible to be suddenly transported between America and Europe in just a few minutes, and yet this was possible with the U.S. space shuttles.

Remember Thomas Edison's comment "New ideas will never end."

The possibilities of the Future are limitless.....

Chapter 7 - Notes

Bibliography

Basadur, Min. The Power of Innovation. London, UK: FT Pitman Publishers, 1995

Belasco, James. Teaching the Elephant to Dance. New York, NY: Crown Publishers, 1990

Barnett, Lincoln. The Universe and Dr. Einstein. forward by Albert Einstein. New York, NY: Bantam Books, 1948

Bennis, Warren and Nanus Burt. Leaders: strategies for taking charge. New York, NY: Harper Business, 1997

Bennis, Warren and Ward Biederman, Patricia. Organizing Genius: the secrets of creative collaboration. Reading, MA: Addison-Wesley, 1997

Burns, Tom. The Management of Innovation. Oxford, UK: Oxford University Press, 1994

Conot, Robert. A Streak of Luck: Life and Legend of Thomas Edison. Hoboken, NJ: John Wiley and Sons, 2000

DeBono, Edward. Six Thinking Hats. Toronto, Ontario: Key Porter Books, 1985

Deming, W. Edwards. Out of the Crisis. Cambridge, MA: MIT – CAES, 1982

Deutschman, Alan. The Second Coming of Steve Jobs. New York, NY: Broadway Books, 2000

Drucker, Peter. Managing for the Future. New York, NY: Truman

Talley Books, 1992

----------. Innovation and Entrepreneurship: practice and principles. New York, NY: Harper Business, 1993

----------. Frontiers of Management. New York, NY: Truman Talley, 1986

Einstein, Albert. Ideas and Opinions. New York, NY: Crown Publishers, 1954

Foster, Richard. Innovation. New York, NY: Summit Books, 1986

Hammer, Michael and Champy, James. Reengineering the Corporation. New York, NY: HarperBusiness, 1993

Hope, Janet. Biobazaar: the open source revolution and biotechnology. Cambridge, MA: Harvard University Press, 2008

Hurst, David K. Crisis and Renewal: meeting the challenge of organizational change. Boston, MA: Harvard Business School Press, 1995

Kanter, Rosabeth Moss. The Change Masters: innovation and entrepreneurship in the American corporation. New York, NY: Simon and Schuster, 1983

Koestler, Arthur. The Act of Creation. New York, NY: MacMillan, 1964

Kriegel, Robert. If It Ain't Broke...Break It. New York, NY: Warner Books, 1991

Lacey, Robert. Ford: The Men and the Machine. New York, NY: Little, Brown & Co., Boston, 1988

Lafley, A.G. and Charan, Ram. The Games Changer: How you can drive revenue and profit growth with innovation. New York,

NY: Crown Business, 2008

Land, George T. Grow or Die: the Unifying Principle of Transformation. New York, NY: Random House, 1973

May, Matthew E. The Elegant Solution: Toyota's formula for mastering innovation. New York, NY: Free Press, 2007

Naisbitt, John. Megatrends: ten new directions transforming our lives. New York, NY: Warner Books, 1982

Peters, Tom and Waterman, Robert H. Jr. In Search of Excellence. New York, NY: HarperBusiness, 1982

Peters, Tom. Thriving on Chaos. New York, NY: Alfred Knopf, 1987

Pinochot, Gifford III. Intrapreneuring. New York, NY: Harper & Row, 1985

Potts, Mark. The Leading Edge. New York, NY: McGraw-Hill, 1986

Reti, Ladislao editor. The Unknown Leonardo. Harry N. Abrams, Inc: New York, NY, 1974

Schumpeter, Joseph. Capitalism, Socialism, and Democracy (1950). New York, NY: Harper Modern Classics, 2008

Toffler, Alvin. Future Shock. New York, NY: Random House, 1970

----------. Power Shift. New York, NY: Bantam Books, 1990

----------. The Third Wave. New York, NY: Bantam Books, 1980

----------. Adaptive Corporation. New York, NY: Bantam Books, 1985

Trimble, Vance H. Sam Walton. New York, NY: Dutton Books,

1990

Wallas, Graham. The Art of Thought. London, UK: Jonathan Cape, 1926

Waterman, Robert, H. Jr. The Renewal Factor. New York, NY: Bantam Books, 1986

Watson, Thomas J. Jr. Father, Son & Co. New York, NY: Bantam Books, 2000

Womack, James P. The Machine that Changed the World. New York, NY: Scribner, 1990

--- end

Possible: A Guide for Innovation

Book Notes:

Possible: A Guide for Innovation

Book Notes:

www.ingramcontent.com/pod-product-compliance
Lightning Source LLC
Chambersburg PA
CBHW051646170526
45167CB00001B/357